Off The Beaten Track

Alex Askaroff

Front cover image
Piddinghoe, East Sussex, by Alex Askaroff.

The images in this publication are by permission of Alex Askaroff, the people named in the stories that supplied them, or are in the Public Domain. If any copyright holder believes this is not the case we would be pleased to be informed for future editions.

Author's Note

Astonishingly, I have had over two dozen books published, some by American publishers, and some by English ones. However, we are in a new age and for the very first time, with the help of the largest book publishers in the world, Amazon, I have completely self-published this work. I have laid out every word on every page, inserted every image, comma, and full stop. I have spent an age with Amazon and their great publishing tools. I do hope the effort has been worthwhile. Amazon, who now advertise and supply my books worldwide, have supported me every inch of the way and have made this amazing step possible.

Off The Beaten Track

Alex Askaroff

The rights of Alex Askaroff as author of this work have been asserted by him in accordance with the Copyright, Designs and Patents Act 1993.

© 2020 Alex Askaroff

All rights reserved. No part of this publication may be reproduced, stored in a retrieval system, or transmitted, in any way or form, or by any means, electronic, mechanical, photocopying, or otherwise, without the prior permission of the author.

ISBN: 9798621671662

British Library Cataloguing in Publication Data.
A catalogue record for this book is available from the
British Library.
BISAC Subject Headings: Biographical
CIP Library Reference: Biographical

For other publications by Alex Askaroff visit Amazon

Acknowledgement

Many thanks to my daughter in law, Corrinne Askaroff, who corrects my grammar and spots the silly mistakes I make. My books are better due to her hard work and diligence. To John Vincent who loves my books so much I made him read through the first proof of this one. That will teach you mate. But really thank you so much John. And finally to Malcolm Lawson for the final read through. Without all their efforts to correct my English there may have been a lot more foul words in this book!

Please bear in mind that this is a production brought to you from the heart rather than a cold unfeeling editing desk. Finally, before we get started, I must tell you this book is written in 'United Kingdom' English, so all the spelling mistakes are absolutely positively on purpose. That's my story and I'm sticking to it. Enjoy it in the same spirit that it was written, with a smile and a happy soul.

Dedication

I could never write these books without the encouragement from so many of you from around the world. When a message arrives from our new 'electronic' world it lifts the spirits and speeds me on. I knew I had struck a major chord when one reader told me that she had moved house to be near my stories!

This book is dedicated to my readers and family. They are the blood that pulses through my heart.

CONTENTS

Introduction

Little Betty

Sweet Charity

Crazy Chloe

Black Shadow

End Of Empire

Pinch Myself

Lucky Gordon

Love The Job Or Die Trying

April 2019

Lilacs & Lilies

Emergency Service

I Should Be So Lucky

Off The Beaten Track

Things We Remember

Scooter Girl

William Terriss

Equinox

Bondolfi

Winter Work

Epilogue

Whatnots, Thingys & Diddlydoodas, The Longest Introduction Ever!

"Oh you must always fill in the holes, Alex."
"Why, Maud? They are only small and who's going to notice them in the cushions?"
"Silly boy. If you don't fill in the holes the Devil might spring out! Then you'll be sorry!" I looked at Maud, who at 102 was by far my oldest customer. I smiled. Even after 40 years she could surprise me. She had bought her machine new in 1936 to celebrate the birth of her first child and had used it ever since. A cracking Singer model 99k sat proudly on her table as if it were listening to the conversation and loving every second. "I've been sewing on that old banger since I was 20 and she has never let me down."
"You don't have to tell me, Maud, I've been looking after it since I was a kid and I have the feeling in another 100 years it will still be sewing like new."

As I went to leave, Maud made the huge decision to see me out. At 102, every decision is huge. She announced to the room, "I am going to stand up now! There's still a bit of life left in these old bones."
Her daughter (who was 82) came around to help her up. "You're still a game old bird aren't you Mum," she shouted at her.
"Oh yes darling, a bit gamey smelling, too!" Eventually, with massive heaving, Maud started to rise. She was almost upright when she let out the most tremendous FAAAART. She looked at me triumphantly with a wicked smile. "Happens every time my dear boy." Her daughter ignored her as if nothing had occurred but toddled round the room and pushed the French doors, leading to the garden, open. I

started to giggle but suddenly Maud wobbled. Before I could move she dropped straight back down onto her seat with a thump. "Well, that was a waste of time and energy, wasn't it! Actually Alex, now that I'm back down here, I don't think I'll see you out."

"No worries Maud," I said, still smiling like a little kid who had seen something really naughty. "If you get a chance, go and sit in the garden later" I added. "It is another day made in Heaven and not to be missed. The weather forecasters are threatening storms. They will break this week of fabulous sunshine."

"Ah, I will do exactly that. I'll make a grand expedition to the summerhouse for afternoon tea. Remember Alex, it doesn't matter what those idiot forecasters try and scare you with, they can't take this beautiful day away from us!"

As I drove away I waved to Maud's daughter and purred down the track from their farm in my new Suzuki Vitara 4x4. I thought how my old banger, my Land Rover Discovery, would have left a nice puddle of oil behind.

In front of me lay around half a mile of private track cutting through the thick Sussex farming belt. Time for a break I thought to myself so I pulled over at the perfect spot and relaxed. I often steal precious moments during my day to daydream (I'm sure Professor Clever Clogs has a technical name for it). Somehow a quick break in silence resets my busy brain and allows me to absorb what is going on around me. So often we rush through life and don't slow down to smell the flowers.

2017 was the best Summer that I can remember, certainly since I was a spotty teenager and 'The Great Summer of 76'. It was followed by the wettest, most depressing Winter, which dragged on until mid-April of 2018. Then as if by some miracle (it turned out to be a blast of hot air from Portugal) the temperature went from hardly above freezing, with icicles hanging from the outside taps, to 29 degrees Celsius in the shade. The hottest Spring since 1949 turned up and roasted us to a crisp. My world instantly turned from cold and wet to all the colours of the rainbow as Spring busted out. No one knew that the Summer of 2018 would then go on to break all records.

This picture was taken in March of 2018. No one had any idea (including the weather forecasters) that within a few days the sun would break through and a heatwave would follow.

You know, if you had to choose a colour for England it would be grey. For months of the year, grey skies rule. It means that when the change does eventually arrive, we all get a little over excited. In Spring the woods are suddenly strewn with whites and blues, the parks with crocus of all colours, topped by perky yellow daffs. My road, Willingdon Park Drive, is lined with blossoming cherry trees in pink and white. Best of all, my favourite garden weed makes an appearance, the lesser celandine. They open their bright yellow petals and worship their sun god. It might only last a few weeks but the joys of Spring put a bounce in everyone's step. Miserable old men who never smile, stop to chat to strangers and blow raspberries at babies. 2018 was so hot the lush green downland of our South Downs National Park turned as brown as an African Savana fit for a pride of lions.

As I sat I thought how our world was still turning in its usual chaotic way; death and destruction seemed to be all around. Of course death and destruction has always been all around on this blob of molten iron speeding through space. However, somehow Chicken Licken and his relatives have got hold of the media. They love making every day a 'disaster day'. Having every awful tragedy from around the globe thrown in front of our faces on a daily basis has made life harder for everyone.

In truth the world is more complicated now, and it's not just because I have raced by the 'Big 60' into my old age. Things ARE just more complicated. Now we are surrounded by whatnots, thingys & diddlydoodas that defy my brain. I'll give you an example of everyday life that has become unnecessarily complicated, and possibly one more of the countless reasons everyone seems to look so stressed now.

In Bexhill, I often use the car parks in the De la Warr Pavilion, along the seafront. It is perfect for some of my customers and even better for me as it is opposite Di Paolo's, the best café in Bexhill. Ever since they put parking meters there, you simply walked up to the meter, popped in your pound, pulled out a ticket and went for a lovely cup of hot Java at the café. Not anymore! My first experience of the latest meters was a typical modern horror story.

A feeling of dread came over me when I was confronted by the new machine. It had several panels and key pads, coloured buttons and three lots of instructions! Someone had kindly scratched some of them out. I sighed and went back to the car to retrieve my glasses. I saw that the first thing that I had to do was select the language that I would like to communicate with the machine in! The previous customer must have been Spanish, or maybe it was them that scratched out the instructions after giving up!

My original train of thought had been lost. Now I needed all my brain cells to circumnavigate the minefield that this new parking machine presented. In reality I didn't want to communicate with this money sucking monster. I would love to chop it down and melt it into something useful. I calmed myself and picked English. Part one had been accomplished without too much pain. Then I selected my registration number, easy, I had been driving the same old banger for 21 years, 788 ALX. Oh, its not working. I concentrate and find out that it only wants the first four digits. How do I go back? No! It's switched to Spanish again...

In desperation I looked for another machine (this one was driving me insane). I spotted one on the horizon and made the hike across the car park. I selected English and pumped in my first four digits. Maybe that's how it works! I quickly totted up the number of possibilities, 42 buttons on one keypad, six more on another pad and then there was all the methods of payment, some with names I've never even heard off. A quick calculation shows that there were thousands of possible outcomes to this engagement, most of them leading to a fine. The machine has obviously been designed by a university graduate who slipped into his uncle's parking meter firm. He has somehow convinced the entire company that the way they have been making meters for the last few decades is wrong. What they need is a life sucking MONSTER!

Unless you have a degree the Bexhill-on-Sea parking meters will drive you nuts! Notice the size of the writing on the regulations and the £80 charge if you get anything wrong! Many councils have found revenue from parking, and fines, easy money. Brighton & Hove Council raised around £26 million pounds last year from parking!

I carried on heroically, then noticed a shiny little lens at head height. It was a camera recording my transaction (obviously for prosecution at a later date when I'm cutting it down). I breathed deeply and used all my powers of concentration. Finally I heard the satisfied noise of a ticket being printed. I turned and walked by the old man who was waiting behind me to pay. Does he have a shock in store! Maybe he'll be alright and has brought his lunch with him!

I skipped back to the car triumphantly, if not a little peeved because the price has gone up to £1.50 for the hour. As I got to the car I realised I am now driving my new Suzuki Vitara. It has a different number plate!

Imagine at this point a kettle boiling and me screaming a silent scream. I become Edvard Munch's iconic painting, The Scream. It becomes clear why the first machine has been defaced, probably by a pensioner who hasn't been able to lift their arm that high for years, but has made the extra effort just this once. I walked back to the machine, fuming. I notice that I can receive an £80 fine if I don't get this right. I fly through the second run and bung in another £1.50, slap the ticket on the car and drag my feet to the café.

I was exhausted, defeated by this weird world of gobbledygook. Heaven knows what I had been thinking about before the encounter with the meter but any creative juices had been sucked dry. Joe at the café told me that the customers have been complaining, and he thought he knew who vandalised the machine! A few months later, Di Paolo's, probably due to the parking meters, closed and I lost my favourite café. To my horror the parking machines along Eastbourne Seafront then went contactless and plastic card payment only! You can guess what I said about that! If you guessed something polite, get out of the room!

When I was a just nipper I remember my dad sitting in a haze of smoke. He was watching Tomorrow's World. On the box was the presenter, possibly Raymond Baxter. He was standing at a checkout in one of the new amazing supermarkets that, at the time, were flooding the towns and cities. In Baxter's hand was a small piece of plastic. He made, what dad thought, was the most implausible statement ever made! Something like, "One day, this plastic card will replace money." My dad inhaled one last deep drag from his cigarette and stubbed out the butt on the edge of his glass ashtray, already piling over with fag ends. He let out a huge plume of smoke, adding another coat of stain to the room that he had singlehandedly redecorated with his breath, from its original white woodchip to tobacco yellow. In that haze of smoke he muttered under his breath in his thick accent, "Hell will freeze over first!" No one would believe back then that it would be possible to replace money with a piece of plastic. Hell must be getting close to freezing over!

That's what I'm trying to say about this world being complicated for no reason. A thousand little instances like this that have encroached into our daily lives. The best of all was the clock in my new car. It took no less than five people and a trip to the dealers before someone figured out how to change the time! All this complexity nowadays sucks away our most precious gift; time. I call this age 'the age of anxiety'. Like I said, I'm sure it's why so many people are in rotten moods most of the day, trying to forever catch up with... what? Progress perhaps. Youngsters don't seem to do 'easy' anymore. They thrive on complicated, heads down, thumbs to the ready and bash the phone till it gives in.

My hometown of Eastbourne, which was once the 'retirement resort of the south' seems to have doubled in size in just a few years. It now has a vibrant young community. The whole area is expanding at a phenomenal rate, as country roads turn into housing estates and old shops, showrooms and garages become more opportunities for builders to add new homes. Country roads that I used to travel down with hardly a house in them, are now bursting with new homes, all with extra cars. I now have cameras in the front and back of my car as drivers seem to jump out at me from nowhere!

The other main problem as I see it is that suddenly I'm the old man in the crowd. I can tell you I'm not too happy about that! At night, when the wind comes from the south, Eastbourne smells of kebabs, chips, pizzas and Chinese takeaways. I go to bed hungry from the smells as sirens screech and traffic rushes everywhere. I'm sure our boomtown is trying to catch up with Brighton, a few miles up the coast, which now holds the amazing title of 'The Hippest City' on Earth. I have a cunning plan to avoid the traffic though. I'm going to get a carthorse and a compass and head cross-country, avoiding roads all together. All I'll have to deal with is a few irate farmers!

Now, I also have to cope with that wonder of the modern age, YouTube! Sweet Lord that is a major pain in my life. Let me explain. Sometimes when I call on a customer they hand me a fistful of sewing machine parts, "I got it moving. All you have to do is put these back." Give me strength! Recently a customer handed me a spring: "Don't know where this goes but the machine won't work without it! Tried for two days but it won't pick up a stitch." An hour later I discover the spring came out of his torch, from when he tried to change the batteries in it! To his delight I fix the machine and the torch. And so it goes.

Oh no, doesn't it sound like I have become a 'Moaning Minnie', raging against the modern world. Not at all, I love being on the cutting edge, the thrust of technology. It's more like I'm not a fan of self-service checkouts that, for me anyway, take three times as long as the old fashioned tills used to (as I argue about bags!). Or the complexity of auto shut off cars that turn off just as I want to go. Or the delight of trying to decipher instructions so small they must have been written by an ant with a microscope. You won't believe this but it is true. As I write someone has worked out that there are over 55 million options for tickets on British Railways. See what I mean about crazy!

Mind you there is plenty of amazing new stuff that tickles me pink. Ordering stuff from my computer and getting it delivered the next day is amazing. Plus I get the regular bonus of being told by my Eastern European delivery men in broken English that I have spelt my surname wrong as it should finish in a 'v' not double 'ff's'! Each time I smile while politely thinking to myself of something else ending with two ff's!

I love the colour and vibrancy of working with fabric. Here is Maximillian Masoud Tschalabi. He runs the fabulous Eastbourne Rug Gallery opposite St Mary's Church in Old Town. When I fix his machines I feel like I am in a story from the Arabian Nights. Incidentally I have never once come away from his shop with money BUT I have some stunning cloths and cushions at home.

Buying a pair of glasses is so simple but such a joy. It almost miraculously turns back time so that I can see clearly and carry on fixing sewing machines. For all of human history, with poor eyes, I would have been on the scrap heap. Even better, great coffee is everywhere! I don't know how George Clooney did it but his Nespresso coffee machines are in just about every other house I call on. Yipee. Max, who runs the Eastbourne Rug Gallery, full of the most beautiful Persian silks you could ever imagine, made me a small coffee that was so powerful I was jittery for a week! I swore to myself that the next time I called to repair his machines I must not have another. You guessed it. I did!

I seem to be just as busy as ever. The phone still rings off the hook and the computer overheats with requests. Adam Shalet from Love Productions needs some words for a voice-over for the latest BBC series of the Great British Sewing Bee. I adore the programme and have helped them before, even appearing in an episode. So I kindly oblige and write down what they need.

The Repair Shop, a great new series that brings old family heirlooms back to life, wants help. Sian Bantock, the assistant producer on the show is a dream, so full of excitement she almost burns my ear off while talking to her. I help out where I can and deliver bits to their farm workshop in West Sussex. When Sian spotted me she squealed like a kid and rushed over. I showed Dominic Chinea, one of the stars of the show, a few tips on how to bring the machine they were repairing back to life. It was an 1890 Willcox & Gibbs chain stitch, which I love. I wished them luck and hit the road. Over the next few weeks I make a handle and send more parts, guiding Dominic through the tricky but exciting job of sewing machine renovation. All this is done for free, the silent helper in the background, and I am happy to do it. I get a little buzz when I watch the program knowing that once more I had silently helped with making an episode work seamlessly.

A new antiques quiz show in Bristol wants me as a contestant. I politely tell them where they can shove that! Rosemary from the WI pleads, "Talk about anything you want, just turn up. Our women love you." I know from experience her short talks turn into marathons and politely tell her I'll sleep on it (for a decade or so). The Rotary Club are asking if I could pop up to Buckinghamshire and do a talk on the Luton Hat Industry for them. Once more I politely 'think about it'.

However, Michael Buerk was filming a new series called How The Victorians Built Britain. I can't start the car fast enough to race up to London for the filming. It turns out that Michael and I have the same sense of humour and we got on like a house on fire. Filming takes far longer than it was supposed to as we keep mucking it up. The bonus was that we were filming in one of the greatest places on Earth, The London Sewing Machine Museum, owned by my old friend, Ray Rushton. Before long we were throwing instructions at the director and crew, telling them what we shall film! The programme was a great success and had one of the highest channel ratings the week it was shown.

BBC Scotland were doing a piece on the amazing Kilbowie Factory that made Singers for nearly 100 years. Vicki Watson, who is assistant producer for TVi Scotland, informs me that I am known as The Sewing Machine Guru. Well, they had me didn't they! I mean flattery always works (whatever people pretend). I was happy to write anything they wanted and appear in their picture. Filming took an age. The results, which were broadcast worldwide, showed the enthusiasm so many people have for my remarkable trade.

Here I am filming at the world renowned London Sewing Machine Museum in Balham High Road, London. I am with the famous presenter of the show, Michael Buerk. We had such a laugh filming that it took twice as long but no one cared! We had just filmed a scene here and completely messed it up. Neither of us noticed until the producer shouted CUT.

Riot Film Group follow me around for a month for a short film, 'Alex's Stitch in Time'. My customers got quite a shock when I turned up with a film crew, but they loved it as much as I did. It went on to win the Best Short Film Award at some sort of event. They are delighted. Who knew a fat old man fixing sewing machines would be so entertaining! I think it's still going strong on YouTube.

Sewalot.com, my website on the great sewing machine pioneers, is still the most visited website on the planet for antique sewing machines, which constantly astounds me.

However, from that I get many requests for publications from around the world and enthusiastically scribble down all sorts of sewing machine history for them. I don't know how long it will last as my energy drops each month I age. Depressingly, everything takes longer with more effort. Still, I doubt if there are many sewing machine engineers that have had seven No1 New Releases on Amazon! That still amazes me.

I wish they had taught us about youth and time at school, when cuts and scrapes seemed to heal in seconds, bones in a few weeks and our energy was endless. If they only taught us how fast it all goes, how quickly those aches and pains move in and stay, maybe we could have enjoyed our precious youth instead of rushing through it. How I would love to run and jump, play sports and stay up until the early hours like I used to. Now I might be up at midnight, but it's only to go to the loo and take pills! Not quite so much fun! Still that's the way of the world. Can you imagine how helpful it would have been if a teacher had told us that the greatest asset that we will ever have, is not the position we climb to, nor the wealth that we acquire, but our youth! We had to find out for ourselves when it was all over! Now I pop the doc's medicines like a good boy and learn from my amazing customers, who constantly remind me that old age is no place for the weak-minded!

The best one was Rosemary at the convent in Uckfield. I had been talking about all my aches and pains. As I left she looked at me and said these immortal words, "Alex, remember one thing, no one gets out alive!" Of course she is right but we all choose to ignore that fact for as long as we can. I thought for a long time about calling this book, No One Gets Out Alive! Then I thought others may not see the funny side of it and stuck with my original title.

Recently I have noticed something extraordinary. During the last few months I have been taking my watch off! Especially when the grandchildren come around. Now, for someone who has spent his life anchored to the ever-ticking seconds of a wrist watch, this really is an extraordinary step. Over the years I had bumped into endless old folk and noticed that some of the most contented ones never seem to worry about the time! Subconsciously I have been doing the same thing, pottering away in the garage or workshop with no regard for the hour. That one single step has been a revelation to me. If I could point at one thing that helps you enjoy life a little more, that would be it. Simple but profound, do not be a slave to time. You can never master it, but with a few simple steps, you can almost ignore it.

I still adore writing down my travels and telling everyone about some of the amazing customers that I come across, hidden away along the old tracks in the Sussex folds. I get an enormous buzz when, out of the blue, a customer transports me into their world and drags me with them back to the favourite time of their lives. I've never figured out why people tell me these wonderful tales, but I am always grateful.

I genuinely have no idea if this will be my last book. I said that when I wrote 'Have I Got A Story For You'. Then along came 'Glory Days' which also went down a storm. Maybe it will, maybe it won't. As long as I have the energy and the phone still rings, my options are open. And, for someone who has spent his life rolling down the tarmac, the road is always whispering to me.

Against every prediction from every 'expert', sewing is on a roll. From Steam Punk to period re-enactments, the rise of the prom dress (and now pre-proms too) to quilting as a major hobby, sewing is bigger than ever. The problem is that there are customers who seem to think phoning at midnight on Sunday is perfectly fine when THEY HAVE a sewing emergency!

Carola Van Dyke is a fabric artist who supplies stores like Liberty in London. Her work is inspiring. I never understand where artists get their ideas from but these multi-coloured fabric animal heads are on walls all over the world.

Upcycling is on a roll as well. It's the new recycling that we all used to do! There has been a surge of young entrepreneurs wanting to craft quality goods, like the old days. That has also bought a boom to the old sewing machine trade. Bunting, that disappeared back in the 1970's like gingham material, is also back like a rash. To top that, for the first time that I can remember, there is no set fashion trend. I mean, who would have thought that superstars would wear beanies on television, and ripped jeans to Buckingham Palace! Luckily I'm in the middle of all this wonderful creativity, running around repairing the machines that make all this weird and wonderful stuff. They say there is no rest for the wicked, but in truth there isn't the time to be wicked, and as my customers remind me most weeks, there's plenty of time to rest when I'm dead!

Actually, let me tell you a little fact. I reckon that I'll be busy for about five years after I am dead! The phone will ring, "Can Alex call on Tuesday?"
"I'm afraid he died!" My wife will say.
"Oh, can he come Thursday then?"
"Alex is dead!"
"Well, I can do any day next week if that is better."
"I'll tell you what," Yana will interrupt, "I'm having a séance next Friday. Perhaps I can get some tips off him!"
I've always said to Yana, when 40,000 women are crying over me at the crematorium it's only their wonderful sewing machines that they're concerned about! One of my customers assured me that she would still come round and check to see if my car was there! Now that's commitment.

Speaking of my customers, they are the same assortment; the mad, bad and bonkers, some of them running very successful businesses I might add. My angels and demons are in much the same proportions. Luckily I would say it is about 99% angels with just the odd demon to keep me grounded. I swear some nights the old bats creep into my dreams and turn them into nightmares.

Here is Andy who runs Sew & Sew in Uckfield. The haberdashery is a joy to visit and is like stepping back in time to a shop from the 1970's. A million buttons, zips and ribbons are stacked from floor to ceiling. Wool is also having a big revival with many new patterns and colours plus computer printed dyes that make up patterns from the ball of wool as you knit.

Sadly, lots of my favourite customers have once more bit the dust. Both Geoff and Brian, the Birling Gap fishermen have gone to the happy fishing grounds in the sky. I used to repair their machines in their net shed, perched almost on the edge of cliffs at Birling Gap. They used to use a specially adapted industrial sewing machine to sew lead-filled rope to the bottom of their nets. Their workshop looked out over the cliff faces of the Seven Sisters and the rolling downland behind. It was possibly the most beautiful place on Planet Earth. I would stand outside their shed and let the sweet smell of the sea salt wash over me, thinking I was in paradise. Their lobster boat, the Sharlisa, (named after their daughters Sharon and Lisa) has been pulled up from its moorings and disposed of (it was the only boat that had permission to be on the beach at Birling Gap). I often used to gaze out to sea and see it bobbing up and down on a silvery wave, knowing those two old salty sea dogs would be sitting in it, hardly a word spoken for hours on end.

David Piper, the superb shoe maker up on the high pavement at Hurst Arms, had bravely fought our great plague, cancer, but succumbed. He made my mum's Paris pumps and my dad's heavy brogues when I was a kid. As soon as I had learnt my trade I looked after his big leather machines. At 73, death had come to call for him. One more of my precious customers had bit the dust and the skills that he had learnt from his father had died with him. His trusty German Adler sewing machine was taken to the last boot repairers in Eastbourne, Rod, down in Langley Road.

But then there was Maud, who could ruffle the curtains with her farts, still going strong at 102! Apparently she had diphtheria as a child, leaving her with a weak heart! During WW2 she would walk with her friend, Flossie, across the fields at Hampden Park, past the Lottbridge Arms and the brick works where Highfield Junior School is now. She walked by all her friends' houses, the Atfields, Richardsons, and Tugwells. Then off to Stone Cross to pick peas for the farmer to earn a little cash. On the way back they would pass the German internment camps, often stopping to buy trinkets from the POWs who made gifts out of any scrap they could find to sell for a penny.

Maud, with her weak heart, had gone on to outlive every person she knew as a youngster and, as she liked to point out to me, four of her doctors! The people she would talk to on her journey to pick peas are also long gone, ghosts remembered now only by some of the road names around the Hampden park area.

Over the coming journey together we shall explore a few more spellbinding customers. Their true tales will jump from the following pages. We will also uncover some unusual ancient history. And, as Maud always reminded me when I visited her, no matter what age you are, look forward with the eyes of a child and you won't go far wrong.

Like many of my customers, Maud lived well off the beaten track and my new Suzuki Vitara was proving ideal for these kinds of visits. However, the car's handling along these types of path was, as yet, untested. She drove beautifully along normal roads but I needed to find her limits for the approaching winter. The tracks I travelled would turn from dry and dusty to slippery and slimy as the mud, mixed with water, becomes something known to the locals as 'Sussex butter'.

My beautiful old Land Rover that I had owned from the age of 38 up to 61 had to go. She had put up a brilliant fight, but the roof leaked and there was often as much water inside as out. The heater was bust, so even with double socks I froze all winter. Everything was old, heavy and hard to use. I'm sure I could have kept a goldfish in one of the front headlights! The paint had completely worn off in places where she had been washed so many times. She had a quarter of a million miles under her bonnet and smoked worse than my dad. My garage mechanic had warned me that she would never pass the new emission tests. I knew that there was no way out for her. It was a sad day when I had to let her go under the latest Government scrappage scheme. If I was a farmer with some spare land, I would still have her, covered in old canvas in the corner of a barn somewhere, waiting for the day that I won the lottery and had her converted to electric! Still, that old girl will live on forever in my books and in my heart.

My lovely old banger had to go one day. She did well carrying me and my tools for over 250,000 miles along the old tracks of Sussex. I have never been in a car that was more comfortable. I was 38 when I bought her. The salesman told me that I was driving away in the best car in the world. When I was 61, and still driving around in it, I thought about ringing him to tell him that he was right!

I sat quietly pondering life in my new car, around the corner from Maud's place. However it was time to get back on the road. I pressed the start button and listened to the engine purr under the bonnet. I felt like I was a million miles from anywhere. It was a beautiful sunny day. You know, one of those sleepy quiet days where Mother Nature seems to recover. In the shimmering distance I could make out the steeple of Catsfield Church. A row of electricity pylons, supporting a necklace of cables, pricked the burning blue above. Beneath them, the vibrant green hedgerows were cut by blazing yellow fields in full bloom. Sussex had become the colours of the Brazilian flag, yellow, green, and blue. I pulled my sunglasses from the dashboard and slid them onto my nose and turned the radio on. Mr Blue Sky was blaring out of the surround sound. How perfect! I turned the volume up and surveyed the track in front of me.

I was alone, just fields in every direction. I suddenly remembered it was along a track much like this that I had once tested my brand new Land Rover along. Time to do the same with my new Vitara I thought. I revved the engine, selected sport mode, and pressed the button to engage all four wheels. For one last moment all was calm. In the heat I looked down at my glistening arms. I pushed my glasses a little further onto the bridge of my nose and in the silence took a slow deep breath. Then I floored the throttle! For a heartbeat the car stayed where it was as the wheels span, it rocked and shuddered on the spot. Suddenly it gripped and catapulted forward, blowing a hole in the dust storm that I had just created. I flew down the track, slipping sideways around the corners. Inside the car, as the music boomed, I could hear a thousand stones hitting the wheel arches. Half a mile later I touched the handbrake and slid sideways into a clearing. I looked back to see a serpent of dust hanging in the windless air above the track. I smiled. Wow that was fun. Well, she had to have her baptism of fire someday and an open track, miles from anywhere was the perfect place. She had performed flawlessly. From that second I knew she would take me down every bumpy pot-holed farm track and slippery back path that I made my living along.

I dropped the car back into economy mode and pulled out into the lumbering traffic. God have I got the best job ever! Some people spend a lifetime chasing their dreams. I realised some time back, I was living mine.

Come on everyone, hang on to your hats and look out Sussex! We're on our way…

Queen Victoria often pops in for a little sewing and a cup of tea. Actually Carole Allman is a re-enactment specialist and makes many of her costumes on authentic machines from the era. Here she is with an 1860 Shaw & Clark machine sewing braid for her evening dress.

Little Betty

I was running late and felt like the rabbit out of Alice in Wonderland. My date was with Betty Langley, all 91 glorious years of her. If she stood on one of her cake tins she could almost make five feet. I pulled out of Sunstar Lane in Polegate, straight into a mass of traffic heading along the A27. Luckily I'm a sneaky driver, 61 years of living in the same town I'd learnt every back road and shortcut.

I arrived on her doorstep panting, with my rucksack slung over my shoulder and workbook tucked under my arm. "Well, well, well Alex. Never thought I'd see the day you arrived late! I can usually set my alarm clock by your timing."
"Oh it's the traffic Betty. The last few years it's gone mad. I've decided to get rid of the car. I'm going to buy a cart horse and a compass, then go cross country! Still I'm here now and ready to work. Are you still sewing on that old banger your mum left you?"
"How very dare you! That's my pride and joy," laughed Betty, as she took my workbook and shoved me into her kitchen. "I'll reheat your coffee. It's been sitting on the side for 15 minutes. I've a lovely slice of fruit and nut for you that I made yesterday."
"Can't touch it Betty, I'll have gut rot for days. I'm an old man now. I can't eat nuts and dried fruit together!"

"Oh dear, we'll just have to christen the Victoria sponge that I just finished icing."

"Nice one Betty. Your sponge cakes are simply the best." I sat down and got to work on her machine.

"Blimey, your machine hardly turns! What have you been up to?"

"Oh I know Alex. My Arthur would kill me if he saw how I treat that old girl. Still he's been gone 30 years now. How I miss him. Did I ever tell you how we met?"

"Was it back during the war, Betty?"

"Not quite, he was wallpapering a room at St Mary's Hospital up in Old Town." Just at that moment the microwave 'pinged' and Betty pulled out a steaming brew for me. "Still two sugars Alex?"

"Oh yes please." All work stopped on her Singer. Well, it had to really. I had a cup of coffee in one hand and a slab of fresh cake in the other!

Betty's tiny kitchen was clean but messy, if you know what I mean. Bits and pieces everywhere, a vase of fading white roses on the windowsill. Above the kitchen sink were two orange curtains fluttering in the cool breeze coming from the open window. There were notes and photos pinned to a board above the small table, with just one chair tucked under it. Cake tins hung precariously above the fridge stacked like badly shuffled playing cards. On the floor was some old floral vinyl that was probably put down in the 1970's. I looked around, one person's life in the most important room in the house. I could live here, I thought to myself before my eyes came to rest on a fading photo of her late husband.

"Arthur was in the Air Force wasn't he Betty?"

"Yes. He enlisted in 1940. They trained him and shipped him out to Burma. I didn't meet him until the 1950's but I can tell you, he had seen some terrible things.

Arthur Langley in 1940

He was a handsome young man having a bit of trouble pasting paper into a corner when I first came across him at St Mary's. He needed three hands really. As I walked by he called to me and asked me to hold the paste brush. I stared at this beautiful young man with pure white hair and lost my voice. I blushed and held his paste brush while he finished the corner. He promised to buy me a cuppa in the canteen at lunchtime. I skipped off sharpish like. Well, I held my breath as I pushed the double doors open to the canteen that day. I looked slowly around the room and there he was sitting at a table, with two cups of tea and a smile as bright as a summer's day. They say no one falls in love at first sight. I can tell you Alex. They do. Mind you, fate may have been playing with us because as we talked it turned out he had been born at No 11 New Road, just off Seaside. The very same house I had spent the war in!"
"How amazing is that!" I replied.

"I know, we laughed about it for years. Anyway, it wasn't long before we rushed up to the Registry Office and married at the Town Hall in Grove Road. We had many happy years together until his time was up. How's the cake?"
"What cake," I laughed back spitting crumbs, with my mouth stuffed.

Betty and Arthur in 1959

I soon got back to work while Betty rushed around to find a picture of her and Arthur together. I could hear her muttering as drawers opened and closed in the living room, her feet shuffling in her slippers as she returned. She showed me a picture of two young lovers from 1959, a year before they married. "Arthur always loved that picture. If you look at the sleeve on my arm you'll see a lump. That's the silk hanky he bought me tucked up there. I never went anywhere without my lucky hanky. When the good Lord took him, the last thing I did was to kiss it and put it in his pocket."

As I left Betty was laughing again. "Bring a shovel next time as I'll be six feet under." She closed the door as I glanced down at my watch. OH MY GOD. I was now running even later… Someone was bound to slam a door in my face before the day was out!

Here I am with Betty. You can see I am no master of the selfie!

Sweet Charity

I squeezed my way down the back road to Herstmonceux Village, avoiding the rush hour traffic. As I pulled up to my customer I saw Penny waiting at the front door. "On time again, Alex. You're the only person I know who I can set my watch by!"
"Just luck and perfect timing," I laughed back. Inside the terraced house was a person's life condensed into every room; photos of old loved ones, gifts and bric-a-brac collected over decades.

I saw the machine sitting on the kitchen table and moved towards it with my toolbox. It was a hand operated Singer, model 99k. One of the finest sewing machines ever produced at the Kilbowie Plant in Scotland. I had recently finished filming for the BBC about Kilbowie and they had trouble keeping me quiet!
"1939." Announced my customer.
"How would you know that, Penny?"
"Easy. My mum bought it shortly after I was born. It was on offer in the Singer shop after it suffered some damage during an air raid. See the damage on the case? The machine was perfect inside but Dad got 10 shillings off. That was some discount back then. Dad was only earning 19 shillings a week at the local dairy."

"Have you ever seen one of those films Alex, where all hell is breaking loose at a hospital during some sort of disaster?"

"Oh yes, loads of them. Power cuts, people running everywhere, usually screaming."

"Well," Penny continued. "I was born during the first air raid on London. Now I can't remember it of course, but Mum told me that she was out shopping while heavily pregnant when all of a sudden the air raid sirens went off. A policeman then cycled up the street blowing his whistle. Well it hadn't been long since that idiot running the country at the time, Mr. Chamberlain, had told us all to 'prepare for war' before the sirens went off. My Mum, shocked by what was happening, obligingly went straight into labour, out on the street! Luckily she was helped to the hospital and amongst all the commotion I popped out. As it turned out the raid was a false alarm. There were lots of false alarms in the first few months, before the real stuff started. I think it became known as 'the Phoney War'"

Penny sat down and continued. "We were both taken home later in the week. My Dad then spotted this machine in the Singer shop window clearly marked 'Bomb Damage'. When he went in to see how bad it was, it turned out the manager was so desperate to get under his heavy cutting table, during the air raid, that he knocked it off the bench. Besides the case being damaged, it was perfect. Later we were rounded up and ushered off to the safety of Cambridgeshire for the duration of the war. It was out of the flight path of Nazi bombers heading for London."

I had been looking after Penny's machine for over 30 years and I knew her mum had used it all her life. Penny frowned, "It seems to have seized up. Probably because of the oil I used last time."
"What sort of oil was it?" I asked, waiting for an answer that I had already guessed from the smell!
"It was olive oil, the only oil I had. Mum always made me promise to oil it every month. Now it has dried like varnish

and nothing works. She would be furious with me if she was still here."

A short while later I had the old sewing machine purring like new. A cup of tea with curdled milk sat on the table in front of me. I was waiting until Penny had her back turned so I could drop it down the kitchen sink. It's a common problem on Mondays with old women who can't shop for themselves. I came up with a cunning plan. "Oh Penny, what are those lovely flowers you have in the garden?" As she turned to look I swiftly moved to the sink and plopped the tea down the plug hole. "Oh that's my neighbour's garden, I have no idea what they are. Now Alex, I can't let you come here for nothing, you must let me pay you!"

"Great Penny, it's forty pounds please."

"OH NO. I haven't got that sort of money! I'm not royalty you know! But I was thinking I could open my charity jam jar and grab a handful of coins for you. What do you think?" I had to smile to myself. I knew that she wouldn't pay me, she hardly ever did. I might have been fixing her machine for 30 plus years but I somehow signed up to a deal; get paid once and look after it free from then on! "No Penny," I said, "You keep them for your charity. You can settle up with me next time."

I didn't get paid but I did get some good company and a great story. As I was leaving I noticed the curdled milk had blocked her sink. I giggled a little. Her problem now, I thought.

She waved me off from her doorway and I looked back wondering how many more of these wonderful old dears are left. People who survived by the skin of their teeth, through thick and thin, and always with a smile. Penny was 'old school', a girl born during an air raid when the whole world was on fire. Still for now, both her and her machine have lived to tell the tale.

I pulled out into the High Street and headed for a factory in Hailsham where I knew I would get paid for my work. Turning up at home with nothing to show for all my effort could be a dangerous proposition!

The Last British Singer

I was lucky enough to bump into Mrs Harmer who had one of the very last British Kilbowie Singer machines. The largest sewing machine factory in the world ground to a halt in 1980 after nearly a century of making superb machines. Out priced and out competed by Far Eastern manufacturers The Singer Company could do little to stop their own demise.

Crazy Chloe

After a lifetime in the sewing trade you would think that I had seen it all. No. Today, Crazy Chloe was going to show me how to abuse a sewing machine in a completely new way.

In the October sunshine I rolled down the hill from Friston Forest. The sun hung low in the bright sky as sheep enjoyed nibbling on the last lush grass that had sprung up in the dewy autumn fields. I was on my way to Honeycrag Close in Polegate and my second customer of the morning. I was a bit wary because I knew Crazy Chloe all too well. She had a reputation in Polegate that actually scared the villagers. She once screamed and threw a bag of dog poo at a dog walker when she saw them leave it hanging on a tree branch. She chased the manager of Barclays Bank up the High Street, shouting about her overdraft. Boy, that woman was tough and knew the value of a penny!

I pulled up outside her pretty bungalow. Her garden was plastered with tiny garden ornaments from her local discount store and looked great. I took a deep breath, no turning back now! Shortly after I rang the doorbell I could see her tiny frame and massive wild curly hair moving towards the door. Last chance to run I thought. "Chloe, how lovely to see you. How are you?"
"Oh don't ask. I'm only alive because I can't afford the coffin! Come in darlin', I've got work for you. Don't mind

the mess. The cleaner broke last year and he doesn't get out of bed till lunchtime now!"

Chloe showed me into her messy life. We made our way around countless obstacles to a table piled high with junk mail. It was post that she could not bear to throw away. Chloe shoveled a hole with her hands, creating a space on the table. I heaved up her old New Home into the space. "Seized solid!" Chloe announced. "Bloody thing, it's 'ardly been a year since the last time I paid you." I quickly interrupted her with a little correction. "Actually it was three years ago Chloe, and last time you paid me it was with half a pot of honey and two marrows. Not exactly a king's ransom."
"Ah, but there were lovely marrows weren't they? Not that I grew them mind," she threw in with a wicked smile. "Now down to business. My baby has seized up solid. Won't make a bloomin' stitch. She was running slow so I oiled her like you told me to, but then it got even worse, then stopped altogether!"

Sewing machine seizures fall into several categories: lack of oil, thread jamming, bearings tightening, gears stuck, shafts out of line and so on. The worst, so I thought until today, is a main top bearing seizure. The top bearings are the largest on a sewing machine and when they go it can be hard work. I could try for a month and they would still never run properly. "Any chance of a nice cuppa, Chloe?"
"Only if you have one sugar! Last time you caused a sugar shortage in Polegate! I'm surprised you're not type four diabetic!"
"I don't think there's any such thing," I laughed back.
"Well there should be!" She added, muttering something else under her breath as she went. I sat in front of the old machine and tried to turn it. It was locked. I mean LOCKED. There was no movement at all, not even the

slightest wiggle. I let out a deep sigh and surveyed my cluttered prison. I knew Chloe would not let me out of the house until her machine was purring like a pedigree kitten. As I looked across the table I saw a half empty bottle of fabric glue. A sudden feeling of dread came over me. I called Chloe.

"Um Chloe, what oil did you use on your sewing machine?"
"It's right there on the table you pillock. Lost your eyes hav' ya'!"
"Chloe. That's glue!"
"Don't be such an idiot," she said grabbing the bottle. She held it up at an angle to the light and tried to read the label. Then she toddled off to find her glasses. I could hear her swearing like a drunk sailor in the other room. She sheepishly returned. "Do you think that is the problem?"
"I'm pretty sure it is Chloe. The reason it slowed in the first place is that you had the motor switched to half speed. I suspect you then glued the moving parts together to make sure it never works again!"
"NOOOOOOO." She howled. "NOT MY BAAABY. You have to save her," she wailed in desperation. "Look I'll give you two sugars, no, three. I'll give you the whole bag. I've got loads!"
"Let me see what I can do Chloe. Now if you can get me four sheets of kitchen roll. Not one piece cut into four like last time, I'll get to work." I had seen she had not managed to get the top and bottom off so she could only have 'glued' the side needlebar assembly. Chloe shuffled off as quickly as a witch on bonfire night and I got down to work.

An hour later the New Home was stitching like new. I had taken the needlebar out and scraped every last bit of glue away. Then I had carefully reset the whole machine, including the half speed setting. I left with a large muddy pumpkin, a jar of blackberry jam, half a pot of oil, sorry, fabric glue, and yes, you guessed it, some sugar poured into a plastic Chinese take-away container (I knew I'd never get a whole bag). No mention of money was made or forthcoming. I did not have the guts to ask for any. Visions of the Polegate bank manager running for his life always stopped me from trying.

Chloe waved me away with the words. "I 'ope I don't see ya' again luv'. Enjoy the pumpkin. I nicked it from the allotments the other night! Same as your marrows last time." She howled with laughter and slammed the door.

I put my stolen goods on the passenger seat and pulled out of Honeycrag Close. Sweet Lord I love this job. No money, countless crazy customers, and the most life affirming, soul fulfilling way to grow old. I knew that as sure as the sun rises it would not be long before Crazy Chloe did something else stupid to her baby and I would be back!

You can see how Chloe made the mistake. Here is her glue and a bottle of sewing machine oil. I did nicely out of it with a huge pumpkin. I was not sure to believe if she had stolen it or if she was just kidding. Interestingly it is sitting on an 1866 Wheeler & Wilson treadle base which lives in my garden.

I never knew when I bought this cart that it was something really special, when I turned it over to do some repairs I found an old badge dated 1893 from Smith & Son of Herstmonceux. They were the original trug makers who supplied Queen Victoria. No one knew that they also made these Sussex Carts.

Prawning amongst the gullies and rock pools beneath the Sussex cliffs has been a passion of mine since a kid. My trips are less strenuous now but I do get visitors.

My daughter, Sarah has a lovely old Bernina once owned by Doris Day. Unfortunately it was Doris Day that ran the Polegate Post Office and not the famous actress.

Autumn in England is something special. Here are the geese migrating to their winter feeding grounds. They are 'honking along' above Sarah at Alfriston.

Tuesday 19th June 2019 started like any other day but as darkness fell a storm erupted the likes no one in living memory had witnessed before. Over a thousand lightning strikes an hour shattered the night for six hours. Here is Eastbourne taking a hammering. It made me think of a battle raging and perfect to include the warriors fighting on the roundabout at Battle, where the most famous fight in English history took place in 1066, The Battle of Hastings.

Black Shadow

"I'm so glad you're here, Alex. It's Percy's birthday today but he is so depressed it's making me cry. It's as if a shadow has come over him and he just won't snap out of it."

"What's happened?" I asked, as I put my toolkit down in the hallway.

"The doc's told him he has a weak heart and its knocked the stuffing out of him. For the last month he has just sat in his chair watching the gogglebox, hardly saying two words between breakfast and supper. It's his birthday today and he hasn't even opened his cards. I'm so worried. I just don't know what to do?"

"Don't you fear, Iris, I'll have a word. You put the kettle on and leave him to me. I'll have a chat before I pop up and fix your old Frister sewing machine."

I took my coat off and slung it over the white painted bannister, noticing a row of old photos going up the stairs. They were mainly war photos of Percy when he was in the Royal Armoured Corps, on the tanks in Africa during WW2. Young fit men all looking excited and handsome, all ready for action. In the first frame was a young Percy. He couldn't have been hardly 20 and yet he was already wearing stripes and in command. The enthusiasm and energy almost jumped out of the frame. However, in the other room sat a sad old man, the best years of his life behind him, and now in failing health.

I remember the first time I met Percy. Actually I heard him a good mile before I caught sight of him. I was standing outside Motcombe Motorcycles talking to the owner, Mr Prentice. He had just put a new MOT on my moped, a yellow Yamaha FS1-E. It was a bitterly cold winter's day but a blue sky and bright sun had painted the day in colours straight from the Mediterranean. Our conversation was broken by a rumble in the distance. Like thunder it came, rolling over the hills, getting closer and closer. Then we saw him. It was Percy, riding a Vincent Black Shadow, possibly the most iconic motorcycle ever made. He was wearing a little peaked open face helmet with leather goggles and leather jacket. His trousers were half way up his calf muscles with thin socks pulled up from his leather lace-ups. Up he rumbled and stopped next to my little Japanese squealer (that if you twisted the throttle like a chicken's neck you could just manage 40 MPH, until you hit any sort of incline). "Just topped 112 over East Dean," Percy announced to us as he slipped off his goggles. "It might have been a fraction more but it was icy and the speedo was bouncing around a tad." I looked on in awe at the man and the machine. To a kid starting out on a lifetime's passion for motorcycles, Percy had just become my hero.

I bumped into Percy a few years later, polishing his old bike as I called on his wife. You couldn't mistake the six foot four ex-army man, his posture and physique gave him away. I knew in an instant who it was. To my surprise he recognised me too. We had a chat before I went in to repair his wife's machine and from then on I bumped into him every blue moon or so, when Iris's machine went pear-shaped.

Anyway, I took a deep breath and walked into the living room. Percy was sitting there watching morning TV with a blanket over his legs. In front of him was a small table with an untouched cup of tea and a pile of cards. "Morning Percy," I said with as much enthusiasm as I could muster. "I hear congratulations are in order. It's your birthday." I put my hand out, grabbing his before he could think, and shook it warmly. He looked up blankly, but then a little smile slowly crept over his face. "Still got that piece of Jap-crap, that little yellow wasp of a Yamaha? My old bike went faster in first gear that that thing could go if it was falling over Beachy Head!"

"Ha, you remember it then. I loved that bike, 49cc of pure power. I blew up two engines and never even reached 55 mph on it! I moved on to bigger bikes over the years Percy, but nothing like your old beauty. What happened to it?"

"Had to sell her. I got too old and couldn't get her started. Sad day that, mind you all the days are sad now."

"Why's that Percy?" I asked, knowing full well the answer that was coming.

"Doc's told me I have a weak heart."

"How old are you Percy?"

"Ninety five today."

"Not bad. Any of your old school mates still here?"

"Nope, not the one."

"What about your old pals in the army. Any of them still knocking around?"

"Nope. Bill was the last of the crew to go. He went last July."

"What about any of your old workmates after you came out of the army?"

"You know lad, I don't think there are any left, now that you mention it. What are you getting at?"

"Well, your doctors told you that you have a weak heart, right?"

"Yes, that young whippersnapper. I hardly spent two minutes with him on my last visit. He was so full of it. I can tell you he wouldn't have lasted an hour out there in the desert."

"So let me get this straight," I said to Percy, looking him straight in the eyes. "Your heart is so weak that you've survived a world war. You've survived everything that life has thrown at you in the intervening 70 years or so, and outlived just about every other person from your age group. Am I getting this right?"

"Well I suppose you are lad. When you look at it like that, I think you're spot on."

"In fact," I threw in quickly, "You're probably the strongest person that I know."

Percy was now sitting upright, sipping his tea. "Come to think of it lad you've got a point. I'll prove that little sod wrong. Hey, did I ever tell you the funniest thing I ever saw during the whole war?

"Go on Percy, I'm all ears."

I sat down and prepared myself for a good yarn. I was well aware that these glorious days were all slipping away, as the last of the 'old guard' disappear.

Percy started his tale. "We did a bit of service up around Northolt Air Base during the war." "At the time they were training Polish airmen to fly Spitfires and Hurricanes. Well, we had stopped our tanks for a break and were sitting all over them drinking a quick brew and chomping on our meat paste sarnies before heading off. Suddenly we heard someone barking instructions over the wire fence. We looked around and blow me down, along the tarmac come these Polish airmen. But they're not in planes, they're riding bloody tricycles. I swear on my old mother's grave there were six rows of them, three abreast, pedalling for their lives, with an instructor up their jacksie shouting his head off through a megaphone. 'TURN LEFT' he roared at the top of his voice, and they all went left. Turn right, they all pedalled right. A few crashed into each other with plenty of shouting. It was like a cartoon sketch. We hollered and waved as they trundled by. The funniest thing I ever did see. It turned out they were practicing formation flying. It must have worked as we later found out that their squadron shot down more Nazi planes than any other squadron in the Royal Air Force. Great days those, lad."

Percy suddenly rose, his blanket falling to the floor. "Turn those two bars on the heater off, lad. You know what, I fancy a slice of toast. IRIS LUV, A'VE WE ANY EGGS…AND BACON."

Ah, I thought quietly to myself. I feel my work here is done.

About an hour later Iris popped her head around the corner of the back bedroom where I was finishing off her sewing machine. "What did you do to Percy?" She asked in a whisper.

"What's happened?"

"Just look." She moved the lace curtain back and pointed. Out in the garden was Percy, sweeping the path to his garden shed. Iris quietly opened the window a little and the sound of Percy whistling the tune to King of the Road by Roger Miller came to my ears. Iris whispered again, "Look at his red cheeks. I haven't seen him like that for ages. He loves his old workshop. I can always tell when he's right. He makes a bee-line for the garden shed."

"I can't really take any credit, Iris. I just had a chat with him. Maybe I adjusted his attitude a little. Pointing out the obvious is easy, it's acting on it that is the real secret."

As I left the little terraced house, heading for my next customer, I had no idea what I would find. My good old dad had told me long ago that attitude is everything. How right he was. Nothing is written in stone and if Percy can enjoy his birthday, why not enjoy it. People have always told me that I can work miracles on sewing machines. Luckily I had worked a little one on an old friend who was stuck in a rut.

My God what I would give to be back on that cold frosty morning all those years ago, when we suddenly heard Percy thundering towards us on his Vincent Black Shadow. One hundred and twelve miles an hour! At 16, I never even knew bikes could go that fast!

The Vincent Black Shadow was a phenomenal machine, when most bikes struggled to do 60mph the Black Shadow could easily do over 100mph. It was a monster and pricey too. It was usually bought by the men who had a taste for danger.

End of Empire

As many of you know my Sewalot Site has been the first stop for millions of enthusiasts around the world searching for antique sewing machine information. The site contains decades of research all centered around the humble sewing machine. No finer machines were ever made than at the Singer Kilbowie factory in Scotland. Here is their amazing story.

Forging metal has been a skill shared by peoples and cultures across the world for millennia. In 1850's America, as the fires of civil war rumbled ever closer, Isaac Singer and his business partner, Edward Clark, had taken that skill and turned it into an art form.

They went on to perfect the forging of metal to bring us the first exceptional sewing machine in the world, the Singer Model A. They also used cutting edge technologies to build factories, marching ever forward to become the largest multinational sewing machine company the world had ever seen.

By 1865, as the final weapons of war in America fell silent, Isaac Singer and Edward Clark were ushering in mechanisation on a global scale. They had done it again, designing and building another amazing sewing machine. It would become a universal success, the fabulous Singer New Family Model 12. It would change the lives of millions and usher in a new era of mass production.

The factories needed to build this beauty would spread, firstly across America, then Europe, starting in Mott Street, New York, expanding to Elizabethport, New Jersey, in 1872. The new factories employed thousands of workers and included all the infrastructure, railways and docks, warehousing and container ships. This helped to kick-start the rebuilding of a shattered country, pushing America onward to eventually become the world's first superpower.

Singer would go on to invest millions (billions in today's terms), building factories around the world from Cairo Illinois, to St. Petersburg, Russia, Monza in Italy, Wittenberg in Germany, Bonnieres on the river Seine, France, Brazil and the biggest of them all, Kilbowie in Scotland.

The machines that built the sewing machines (shipped around the world from Elizabethport) were so precise that for the first time parts from any factory could be shipped to another and would integrate perfectly with the sewing machines that were being produced there. It was the first true mass production on a global scale, (forty years before Henry Ford had taken his initial steps to make the Model T).

Kilbowie, built in the cold Scottish hills, was to change a rural valley, on the side of the River Clyde, into one of the greatest powerhouses of industry on Earth, employing at its peak (just before the outbreak of WW1) an estimated 14,000 workers. It would also bring prosperity to the lives of countless other families. Families working in the factories and shipbuilding industries around Clydebank became fondly known as a 'Bankie'.

Mighty Kilbowie, on the curving banks of the Forth and Clyde Canal, became the pulsating heart of the Singer Empire.

Raw pig iron went in one end of the 46 acre site and precision built engineering masterpieces poured out of the other. Eventually, by sea and rail, plane and road, they travelled across the globe to eager customers waiting with open arms. The factory lasted until the original Singer Companies final death knell rang out through the Scottish hills in 1980.

The Singer Company had been on a boom after Edward Clark (in the 1850's) had cleverly devised the first official hire purchase, lay-away, part payment, or instalment plan, allowing just about anybody that wanted a machine, to buy a Singer. The call for their machines was growing at an astronomical rate. Keeping up with this demand, from all four corners of the world, was a major problem for the first ever multinational.

The original idea of factories in Europe was simply to overcome the large costs of shipping heavy iron machines from America, and to get around any import levies or duties imposed by the European powers.

In 1866 Edward Clark's cousin had been sent on a European tour to seek out areas for new factories. He reported back to Clark who narrowed down the ideal locations. In 1867 plans were afoot by Clark to send George McKenzie (who was general manager of The Singer Sewing Machine Company and later President) to Scotland, to prepare the way for one enormous factory instead of their smaller ones.

In the 1860's, 70's and 80's Singer was running several smaller sites in Scotland (mainly based around Glasgow). There was a site at Love Loan that was building complete machines for European distribution (from boxed parts shipped over from America). There was the Bridgeton Site (opened in 1871) which actually made complete industrial models (plus the model 12 and 13 'New family'). There was the foundry at Bonnybridge some 20 miles away, and another at Govan Street in Glasgow.

The Kilbowie site had great potential, and as McKenzie was of Scottish descent, he was the perfect negotiator for the job. The plan was simple, integrate all these smaller plants into one perfect sewing machine manufactory capable of expanding with the market.

The factory needed as many natural resources as possible. Kilbowie offered these in abundance. Coal, steel, and seemingly endless forests for the cabinet-makers to craft the wooden shells of the sewing machines. Then there was the mighty River Clyde, where huge ships could carry Singer's stock across the world. Access to railways from the city of Glasgow just nine miles away, and major road links to the rest of the country, were another bonus.

An explosion in growth was to happen to the tiny rural hamlet as the first sod was lifted with a silver spade by George McKenzie in the spring of 1882.

The factory would be powered by the latest 'cutting edge' steam technology. Puffing chimneys would replace the tall pines and steel rails would bring screeching trains shuddering in 24hrs a day.

784 automated machines would cut and make the screws, nuts and bolts, 182 more would make just the needles.

Huge tubs of whale oil would quench and harden the hot steel shafts. Every facet of production would be handled in one massive plant with 57 separate departments and over two million square feet of factory floor. Some workers found themselves walking up to 20 miles a day, to, from and around the gargantuan plant!

As the Singer model 12 went into production a population boom was to follow as farmer's sons left the hard toil of the land for the heavy thumping of the anvils. The Singer models, 13, 15, and 17, soon followed, all for the first time with the Singer name emblazoned across the arm of the machine.

The main contract for building was won by McAlpine's with their first major contract. Robert McAlpine soon split with his partner (Richmond) and took the contract on alone, using over 20 million bricks from his own brickworks. Robert McAlpine's firm later became Britain's largest road builder.

The Kilbowie plant would not only have the latest machinery inside but it was also protected by fireproof walls of brick, iron and steel, incorporating a full sprinkler system. The factory was impossible to burn.

By 1884 the monster was breathing fire from huge melting and smelting plants as the pig iron was hauled in.

The factory slowly evolved rather than open officially with pomp and circumstance. A monster rose noisily out of the Scottish earth and kept on growing for decades.

Production was slow at first and more trains were put on to bring fresh hands to the furnaces. All the effort paid off because adverts boasted that eventually over one million complete machines every week were being made at Kilbowie by a highly trained and skilled workforce unparalleled on the planet.

In a time of deprivation and mistreatment by the ruling elite, Kilbowie broke the mould. A strike by the women in 1911 (before the suffragettes were even a party) brought benefits. Their courage changed the workforce for the better, though equal pay was still just a dream. The workforce had their own cooks and staff, their own playing fields and sports teams, social clubs, dance halls and even beauty pageants. All-in-all a marvel beyond all description and all to feed an ever hungry demand for the humble sewing machine.

Unfortunately Isaac Singer (the little runaway who had lived on his wits, scraping a living from the dirt), was only to see the beginnings of a mighty dream being built in the north lands of Britain. Isaac died in July of 1875 at his palace in Paignton called Oldway. However his dream did not die with him, eventually leading to one of the mightiest factories on earth at Kilbowie.

At the factory it was not uncommon for three generations of the same family to work side by side as the knowledge and skills were passed down the generations.

Kilbowie would survive two World Wars, but not the ever creeping expansion of throw-away plastic from the emerging economies. The last sewing machine came off the assembly line in June of 1980. Later that year the great factory finally closed its doors. It was abandoned, and finally demolished.

The largest clock tower in the world that summoned the whole valley to work each day was demolished before the remaining workers eyes. Many cried. It was melted down and sold as souvenir ashtrays and other bits of tourist tat. The mechanics of the clock were shuffled away to America never to be seen again. Many of the workers (who had taken over from their fathers and their fathers before them), kept bits to remember the business that had brought employment to generations of working families and changed a country.

The collapse of the shipbuilding industry coincided with the closure of the Singer plant in 1980. For a generation Clydebank became a ghost town. It was the end of an era. The end of a dream, and the end of the British sewing machine industry.

The Singer model 12 was the bestselling sewing machine of the 19th Century. It was the last machine that Isaac Singer had anything to do with and the first machine to carry his name emblazoned across the front arm after his death. It is difficult to imagine a more beautiful sewing machine. This one was hand-built in Scotland around 1884 and cost a year's wage when it was new. Not many people know that it was the Singer Company that invented the first properly

registered hire-purchase scheme in the world. This allowed their customers to pay for the machines over a period from 5 to 25 years.

Our world now turns on plastic and that includes sewing machines. Inside every new sewing machine countless cogs churn away. The day they break is the day that I get a call.

The hooks are the most important part of the sewing machine, they catch the top thread carried by the needle. If the hook isn't perfect the machine won't work.

What is it about flowers? Besides babies and beautiful scenes nothing brings a smile like them. I used a sunflower picture taken by my daughter, Sarah, for the front cover of Glory Days.

I get to visit some amazing properties. Here is Holy Cross Priory on the Blackboys Road where many retired nuns live and Batemans near Burwash where Rudyard Kipling spent many years.

65

Luckily for me my area includes the South Downs National Park. During my working day I'll try and have a break and soak up the beautiful surroundings. Here is Birling Gap, the old smugglers haunt, and Beachy Head. The curving cliffs are one of the iconic Sussex scenes.

Who knew moustaches would come back! Mine would be grey now anyway so I'll give that a miss. I have no doubt that in another life I'd have been a farmer, animals just seem to ignore me which is great for my walks.

I love the sights I see when driving around Sussex. Here are the May Day dancers at East Dean and some magical mushrooms near Jib Jacks Hill in Ashdown Forest. It is easy to understand how A A Milne created Winnie-the-Pooh and other great characters when he was surrounded by so much wonderful inspiration.

I'm convinced there should be followers of signposts like train spotters. Sussex is awash with weird and wonderful posts. You may notice one saying World's End. I bet you never knew that was in Sussex! To top it all I came across this wonderful sign in a pavement. It just made me laugh as you can hardly take a step in this country without treading on a piece of history.

George Brown & Co were Eastbourne's premiere outfitters supplying the wealthy elite of the town. The building, on the corner of Terminus Road, is still there but looks far more mundane today as the Nationwide Building Society.

It's not often that you can pop into Whistler's Mother's house to do a bit of sewing. But that is what I had to do.

Nicola Amies makes childrens clothes under the brand name 'Sea Whistle'. She uses a Janome Memory Craft, a powerhouse of a sewing machine. What is even more amazing than sitting in Whistler's mother's house, in the old fishing town of Hastings, is that Nicola is a distant relation to Hardy Amies, the Queen's dressmaker. It looks like sewing is in her blood. Hardy Amies used to use an ancient Singer treadle machine to create his magnificent works. You can find Nicola's wonderful Sea Whistle clothes online and she is hoping to open a shop in 2020. Amazingly Archie Belaney, known to the world as Grey Owl, once lived just a few doors away.

Pinch Myself

I sometimes have to pinch myself to see if my job is real. Repairing sewing machines has taken me to different people and places for most of my working life. My A-list pass, giving me free 'access to all areas' of Sussex, has been amazing. Each day new, each day different.

As usual, I started at the crack of dawn and headed away from the coast, up country. My first call was a farm in Slugwash Lane, near Wivelsfield Green. A quick repair to an old Pfaff then off to Jose Miguel in Blackboys.

Jose is a specialist upholsterer, dealing with London clients and expensive furniture. His team were carefully working on some antique Georgian chairs for the Ritz Hotel in Piccadilly, London. I repaired two of his industrial Juki walking foot machines and hit the road, stopping for a latte at a new cafe that had opened on the back road to Horam. Well, all new coffee shops in my area have to be tested of course!

At Horam I bumped into Carlos. He had been waiting for me. "I come from the old Romanian Royal Gypsies," he told me in a silky Portuguese accent. "I see you have a strong Russian name, Mr Askaroff (to my amazement he pronounced it perfectly). It is my honour to meet you at last." He nodded his head as he warmly tried to remove my arm with enthusiastic handshaking. I was standing before a middle-aged man of about five foot five inches tall, with long salt-n-pepper hair waving in the warm wind. He had deep penetrating eyes that looked like they could spot a rabbit bolting in the dark. "I need your help my friend." Then he told me about an old Toyota that he had picked up. "It has a few parts missing and I know you are the man." I jotted down what he needed, took his postal address and with more enthusiastic hand shaking and bowing, moved on to my next customer, a massive 20 yards along the gravel drive in the next barn.

Amanda was putting the finishing touches to another of her stunning fairy artworks. The Little White Studio runs alongside May Green Fairies at Horam Manor. Amanda not only creates amazing pieces but teaches others how to do it as well. I fixed her sewing machine and walked out onto the gravel, clutching one of her superb pieces of work to take home. Luckily I had saved Amanda's life by heroically trapping a hornet in a tea cup before releasing it. To show her gratitude I got a great deal on a piece of her artwork. To me it was a steal.

My customer's work is often inspiring. How could I leave her unit without this wonderful piece!

The sun was beating down on the Sussex countryside. The farmland smelt of fresh cut grass and wild honeysuckle, which was growing profusely through the hedgerows. I looked across the fields. They were a Constable painting come to life, strewn with buttercups and daisies, wild orchids and early summer cornflowers. The cornflowers matched the priceless blue sky. Above me the first swifts had arrived from Africa and were dancing on the warm thermals. A Virgin plane was cutting the blue sky in half with a white vapour trail. The ice crystals, caused by the jet engines and the cold air high above, had started above Gatwick. With the plane at its head, it was like an arrow pointing in the direction of Spain. I took a deep breath: still, no time to dilly-dally. I jumped into the car and headed for my next call where yet another wonderful story from long ago would jump out and pinch me.

"'Ello Joan, Leonard told us it would be okay for you to walk out with us," the young soldier said with a big smile. "I don't think so, you cheeky sods. Now clear off the lot of you or I'll tell him." The lads ran away laughing. That's how it all started way back at the outbreak of World War Two, at a post office in the sleepy Sussex hamlet of Bishopstone. But I am jumping way ahead, let me start at the beginning.

I was sitting in front of a beautifully worn Singer vibrating shuttle sewing machine that was made in the mid 1920's. The machine showed all the signs of being lovingly used for decades, and better still it had a story to tell. Like they say, a picture paints a thousand words. The machine was surrounded by telegrams, notes, and newspaper cuttings that my customer and her family had kept with it. Our story is about a young girl and a chance meeting at Bishopstone Post Office that would change her life.

Joan left home at 14 after successfully applying for the job of a domestic at a large manor house in Firle Road,

Seaford. A week after her interview she had packed her meagre belongings and travelled down to the seaside town to start her working life. One of her daily chores at the manor was to walk over the hills to Bishopstone to collect and post the daily letters of the household.

Now, in that strange way fate has of bringing people together, one day Joan was picking up the post when she turned and bumped into a young soldier stationed at the local barracks, on the Tidemills near Newhaven. Leonard was with the Cornwall Light Infantry. He was preparing to leave for Africa when he grabbed the opportunity to post a letter home. That chance meeting led (besides his mates trying to nick his new friend) to a romance that would last a lifetime.

Leonard and Joan became an item. In 1941 Leonard was allowed leave from the theatre of war to return and marry Joan at a local church in Lewes. After the briefest of honeymoons they did not see each other again for four years! Letters arrived, (heavily restricted and censored) as Leonard fought his way through Africa and then Italy. Then one day, just as quickly as it had started, World War Two ended. After years apart Leonard and Joan were finally together and settled in Seaford to bring up their family.

As these epic events took place there was a silent witness, the lovely little Singer that I had come to service. It was a wedding present from Joan's mother Ellen. She had in turn been given it from her mother Katherine in the 1930's. The machine had made dresses and christening gowns, curtains for new homes, and the first clothes for their kids. Through the decades it had silently travelled with just one family, passing from one generation to the next. Each member carefully keeping all the bits and pieces of their lives with the machine, so that one day it could all be revealed like a magic show.

For just the shortest of times it felt as if all the generations were there with me, looking approvingly over my shoulder, while I fixed the machine and made her stitch perfectly once more. While I worked, the latest family member to look after the machine, Jill, the great granddaughter of the very first owner, Katherine, retold the story of the machine and the women that had surrounded it, with letters and telegrams. She recounted the day that Leonard, on just a whim to waste some time, rather than use the barracks post, decided to walk to the post office at Bishopstone to post a letter home. In that moment two worlds changed forever.

Jill's machine is a little time capsule, complete with the original wedding telegrams and cuttings from the local paper, oh and my cup of tea waiting to be drunk.

Lucky Gordon

I am always amazed at where my stories come from that fill the pages of my countless books. When a customer rings, like Robert Keyte Silks, who I only see once in a blue moon, my mind goes into overdrive. The second they start talking I see wonderful images of their sewing room, full of all the silk offcuts lying around the cutting tables, left over from their superb silk ties. They were once in the centre of the silk industry up in Macclesfield and, although I believe they still have their silk printed there, the ties are cut and sewn near Bodiam Castle, on the Kent-Sussex border. I book the call and give them a date. Then my mind slips into 'devious mode' trying to figure out how to get them to give me another bag full of silk offcuts! It's as simple as that. I pick my stories up from here, there and everywhere. Some come from the darkest jungles in South America, some from the Australian Outback, but none came from closer to home than this one.

My neighbour, Ruby, was having tension trouble on her Singer sewing machine and I popped around to adjust it. Sitting on her busy dining room table, full of fabric, wool, sewing machines and trim, was an old photograph. "That's not your Dad is it Ruby? The one and only 'Lucky Gordon' that you've told me so much about?"
"Yes, I thought you might like to see him after all the tales you've heard. How my Dad reached old age is anyone's guess. He got up to so many crazy antics he should have either been killed or locked up. How he managed to wriggle his way through life missing the Grim Reaper right up until he was 81, I'll never know. I guess that's why he was 'lucky Gordon and not 'Blind' Gordon or 'Limpy'

Gordon or something like that. Although with his missing finger I suppose he could have been called 'Stubby' Gordon."

Sidney Gordon Laishley's tale is an amazing one, which stretches over decades. However, we will start his story on one of the most historically important days in history, 6 June, 1944, known to most as D-Day.

Sidney never liked his given Christian name so as soon as he had a chance he swapped it with his middle name and became forever known as Gordon. Gordon had the one key element that Napoleon always searched for in his officers, Gordon was born lucky.

On D-Day, 17 year old Gordon and his comrades from the 1st Dorsets were charging up Gold Beach, trying not to get shot. Their bikes, which they were supposed to get inland on, were washed up on the wrong beach and they were fighting for their lives. He and a handful of his regiment survived the slaughter. The losses were so high that they were later merged with the survivors of the Devonshire and Hampshire regiments.

Gordon lost most of his comrades as they fought their way inland. Eventually just three of them remained! They were being taken out by specialist retreating fighters, especially the snipers. In all the chaos his little group had somehow pushed in front of the main advancing Allied Forces, who had been bogged down on the beaches. After a fierce shootout and with no backup, they ran out of ammunition. The lads had no choice but to surrender and hope they weren't shot.

They were quickly bundled up with other soldiers and sent deep behind enemy lines, stopping only for fuel, supplies, and more prisoners. Several days later they arrived at their destination. They had been taken to a salt mine on the Czech-Polish border in an area once known as Silesia.

At the mine, SS Nazi officers and soldiers were directing the prisoners, immediately putting Gordon and the other men to work. The Nazis needed as much slave labour as they could find as they were hurriedly building rooms, deep down in the salt mines.

The food was rotten and they slept on rags where they worked. The weeks all became a blur. One day a convoy of trucks arrived with soldiers and dozens of crates. As Gordon was moving one of the crates down the mine, it crashed against a wall, slicing his finger off. Gordon screamed but carried on without another word. He had seen what they had done to any injured prisoner! He never complained, just bound it and kept his head down. The alternative was to be shot and dumped. Now and again he would hear a gunshot ring out or a sharp 'barrrp' of machine gun fire and know another prisoner had been killed. The Nazis were particularly merciless to the Polish and Russian prisoners.

Once all the crates were secured the prisoners were rounded up and marched off. Gordon never found out what was in the crates or how they sealed the rooms in the mines.

With the Allied Forces closing in, the prisoners were force-marched on a death march across Central Europe back in the direction of Germany, probably to get them as far away from the mines as possible. There was no mercy shown to the young men. On the march, if a prisoner dropped, the Nazis shot them where they fell. However, Gordon noticed that as the walk went on, the Nazis were running out of ammunition. This was to prove his life-saver, as they just left some of the fallen men to die by the roadside rather than waste the few bullets they had left.

As they marched in complete disarray, Gordon, with his feet bleeding and exhausted, decided he could go on no longer. He would chance his luck or at least die trying. On a sharp bend, with fewer guards to see, he fell to the floor groaning, then rolled down an embankment and stopped motionless at the bottom. He waited for a bullet but none came! Painfully slowly, the convoy passed. He heard the group disappear into the distance. When all was quiet he got to his feet. His luck held, he was free at last.

Gordon might have been free but he had no idea where he was. He decided to walk back to where they had passed an intersection and head west. Sleeping rough and eating anything he could find, he cautiously made his way home. As he got closer to Germany he came across escaped and liberated labourers, soldiers and prisoners. There were American, British, Canadian, Polish, French and Russians, some walking aimlessly, some walking determinedly. Some even carrying packs, probably trying to get home, and seemingly knowing exactly where they were going. However most were lost, just walking and trying to stay alive. Gordon picked up any useful information he could as he went. He found out that the Nazis were in full retreat. He kept heading west. In his young mind he thought that he would skip around the bottom of Germany and hopefully hit Switzerland or France.

Along the way, Gordon came across two disorientated airmen wandering in the same direction. They joined forces and picked up another comrade a few days later. They decided to stick together for safety, then as soon as they came across any Allied Forces they could be returned to their correct units. Every now and then they could hear incredible explosions in the distance. One night they rested up in a partially burnt barn, but as they tried to sleep a terrible stink kept them awake. One of the men moved some straw and found a pile of Canadian airmen. They had been shot and left. The Nazis must have tried to burn the barn but failed. The men decided to move on and walked through the night.

Gordon may have been free but he was not out of trouble. The small group walked for endless days, searching for friendly voices and news of the war. They survived off the land and sheltered with a few approachable people, all the time hopefully getting closer to the Allied Forces and safety. One day one of the lads in the group, a few yards ahead, stood on a mine and just disintegrated in front of them. It was a horrendous reminder that they were still in terrible danger.

In all this carnage there were also lighter moments. One day, Gordon and the two other lads had unwrapped the fabric around their bloodied toes and were cooling them in a pool. Gordon said to his mates that he could murder a cigarette. No sooner had he said that than there was an almighty explosion way off in the distance. About a minute later, out of the sky, a packet of cigarettes fell to the floor, right by Gordon. The lads couldn't believe their luck, and as one had a lighter, they all had a smoke. From then on, Gordon became their lucky charm and the group of lads stuck together like glue. Later they came across the scattered remains of a truck and filled their bags with supplies before carrying on.

On their trudge through the countryside they avoided all large towns, scavenging from the outskirts at night like wild animals. However, a strange thing happened as they moved through southern Germany. To their amazement local people helped them! Families took them in and fed them. Some even gave the men clothes and what little supplies they could spare. Gordon came to realise that the German people were very different to the Nazis he had been fighting. One family even took a photo of the group outside their pretty farmhouse before they parted with hugs and handshakes!

One morning they heard the sound of vehicles. As always, they quickly hid in the hedgerows. A small convoy of trucks came rumbling up the road. To Gordon's shock one of the lads jumped out of cover. He had recognised the American markings on the vehicles. He waved down the trucks and luckily was not shot. It turned out to be a specialist American team who were asking anyone they came across about any mines in the area. The Americans told them some mines contained Nazi loot. Gordon was not surprised!

They were really interested in Gordon and spread all their maps out over one of the truck bonnets. He tried his best but was of little help. He pointed them in the rough direction of where he had come from and told them about any landmarks and towns that he could remember passing. Gordon was stunned to find out it was already May of 1945 and the war in Europe was over! The Americans were incredibly excited and told the lads about an amazing find at Merkers-Kieselbach in April. Escaped prisoners had directed them to the mine near Frankfurt where a team of Military Police were pulling out crates of gold and masterpieces, from sculptures to oil paintings. It turned into the largest treasure hoard ever discovered. Merkers held some of the world's greatest works of art, all hidden in rooms deep in the mine and worth billions in today's money. Even a general had rushed to the mine to examine the amazing find and get his picture taken with the hoard.

Gordon told them about the crates he had unloaded, but he didn't know what was in them. The only thing that he knew for sure was that, in the mine, was his finger! The advance search team radioed back to headquarters and told the group of lads to wait for recovery. They gave them a few cans of bully beef, coffee and bars of chocolate and blasted off up the road, heading for Poland. The three lads knew their war was finally over. For the first time they knocked up a roaring fire and heated up some of the tinned beef to have with their hot coffee. They laughed and talked about what they were going to do now that they had survived.

The next morning they spotted a truck that had orders to collect them and take them to a field hospital. At the hospital, for the first time since D-Day in 1944, Gordon slept peacefully. He came round three days later. The nurse told him his comrades had already been shipped back to their units. They didn't want to wake him when they left but they were sure they would meet up shortly. Gordon never saw either of them again!

One day in the hospital, several officers arrived with maps and interrogated Gordon about where he was captured and where he was taken. He was of little help. They didn't believe how far his initial group had advanced after the Normandy Landings. They didn't believe where he was captured, and they didn't believe his story of escape! After more interrogation it became clear that Gordon was telling the truth. However, as with the Americans, he could not give them any accurate or useful information. They didn't find it amusing when he held up his hand and told them he could prove he was in a Silesian salt mine, as his finger was still there!

With the war over and back with his, now combined regiments, Gordon found out that soldiers were needed to help rebuild Germany. He quickly volunteered. He understood better than most that it was not the German people but the evil regime of Nazism that had fuelled the war. Gordon was posted to a suburb of Berlin and spent the next few years repatriating Germans and getting their infrastructure up and running. While he was in Germany he fell for a young fraulein and soon married. As the years went by, two daughters came along.

By the 1950's, Germany was back on its feet and a lot of the military operations were winding down. Gordon decided it was time to bring his family home. They arrived at Croydon Aerodrome one cold winter's morning and took the train down to his home town of Andover. Unfortunately, when he arrived home, it was not to a hero's welcome.

They soon found out that the feelings towards the Nazis was still raw. His German wife and children were treated terribly by the locals. To make things worse, Gordon, who was now nearly thirty years old, had a twinge of a German accent when he spoke, from so many years working there. It was not long before he got his old local accent back, but the feelings towards them did not soften.

His well-off family were from old Andover stock with proud distant relations like James Watt of steam engine fame, and Officer Laishley of the *HMS* Bounty. The horrible lot flatly refused to see him, or meet his wife and daughters!

That cut Gordon deeply but all that was about to change in the most spectacular way. Always a keen footballer,

Gordon used to enter a weekly newspaper competition called 'Spot the Ball'. In the paper there would be a photo of the players on the pitch with the football removed. For a small fee, you could have a go at guessing where it was. Prizes varied in value, depending on how many weeks the prize had not been won. It was rare to win anyway but 'lucky' Gordon didn't get his nickname for nothing. After weeks of no one winning he scooped a massive prize. With his winnings Gordon had enough money to open a restaurant, then two, then three! He used some of his winnings to pop up to Mayfair in London and buy an enormous Packard motor car. It was so wide it hardly squeezed along the narrow lanes of Andover. That seemed to suit Gordon fine, he was used to close scrapes! His family might have blanked him but he made sure they could no longer ignore him.

By the middle of the 1960's Gordon was swanning around Andover, travelling between his 'eateries' like the king of the hill. He banked at the Royal Bankers Coutts, at 44 The Strand, London, and lived life to the full. Funny really, as by all accounts he should never have made it off the beaches of Normandy or survived the salt mine or the 'death march'. Now he was living the high life! With his made-to-measure Savile Row suits and handmade shoes, even when Gordon didn't have a penny in his pocket, he always looked a million dollars. It was only when he had a crafty cigarette from his pouch of Golden Virginia rolling tobacco that he gave away his old army ways.

Gordon had a natural flair for design. After meeting a like-minded entrepreneur he started another business. With his new business partner Ted, they started Hyde Interiors, which specialised in high-end interior design to the top-end London housing market. In the late Sixties, Gordon moved to Clapham to be closer to his new work in Central London.

In 1967 his daughter Ruby was born (lucky for me as I would never have heard his brilliant story without her).

The interior design business grew and grew and before long his talents were spotted by the celebrities of the day. Adam Faith had his entire property refurbished with their amazing interior designs. Gordon painted ceilings as if they were billowing clouds floating along, with walls of pure silk. Whatever the customer wanted they got. Diana Ross kept an apartment for when she appeared in London and they ensured that every whim of hers was catered for. The billionaire arms dealer Adnan Khashoggi had the best pad in London, decorated with lavish papers in gold and silver. Hidden doors were made to secret rooms and fake books were so expertly painted it was only when you ran your fingers over them that you knew they were not real.

Ruby also benefitted from Gordon's design ability. Gordon would carefully choose and sometimes even make her dresses. If he couldn't find the perfect shoes to accent the dress he would painstakingly paint them to match in patent leather paint. One day, while undertaking a complete refurbishment for the famous golfer, Nick Faldo, and his wife Melanie, Nick noticed that Gordon had laboured breathing. Gordon tried to shrug it off. He had survived everything that the World could throw at him, so a common cold was nothing. Eventually Nick and Melanie were so alarmed they bundled him in their car and drove him to hospital. It turned out that he had advanced pneumonia. If they had not caught it he probably would have died!

When Gordon had recovered enough, Nick and Melanie turned up again and took him back to their newly refurbished home. They looked after him like a couple of dedicated nurses until he was well enough to go home. That summed up Gordon. Everyone who met him respected him.

He always kept his word so that people could rely on him. However hard the job he always finished it and as soon as he was up he returned to work.

Gordon loved a gamble on the lottery. He also loved a barely cooked steak from the best restaurants in town. Fluent in German and with no airs and graces, he was a man that few people could ignore. Although Gordon hardly drunk he did get caught out one night at a new fancy wine bar called Mushrooms, down the A3036 Wandsworth Road. When the owner asked Gordon to try a tipple of his special cherry brandy, he liked it so much he didn't stop till the bottle was empty! Ruby tried to get him home with three steps forwards and five steps back!

As Gordon slowed down, he was always fascinated by any news regarding the mines where the Nazis had hidden their stolen treasure. He knew that there was still billions out there, reports told that at least half of all the stolen loot had not been found. He followed any press releases with eager enthusiasm, hoping to locate the old Silesian salt mine that he had worked in. When Ruby would ask him why, he would laugh and explain that it wasn't really the hidden treasure he was after, it was just his missing finger!

Nigel & Julie Williams are American Civil War reenactors and Julie makes here authentic costumes on a period Willcox & Gibbs machine. A short 50 years ago we were at school together.

The white chalk cliffs at Beachy Head drop dramatically 500ft straight down to the sea. The Beachy Head Lighthouse warns shipping of the dangerous rocks and reefs in the area. It was once manned but is now fully automated. When the weather was bad and boats could not supply them post and supplies would be sent down wires to the men that lived in the lighthouse.

Love The Job Or Die Trying!

I was standing outside a pretty period cottage on the edge of Newhaven, staring at a large weeping willow that was hypnotising me. The long sinewy stems of the willow were swaying like the hem of a beautiful sun-ray pleated skirt. The branches had small green buds bursting out of them. It was the middle of March and spring was fighting against the late winter winds, and winning. The willow was framed by a perfectly blue sky that normally only lived in my dreams. Through the bare tree branches I could just make out the spire of Bishopstone church steeple pricking the pristine sky.

I snapped out of my trance. It was Monday morning and my first call of the week. There is an old tale that tells, if your first customer of the week goes well, then the whole week will follow. Gladys had made sure to tell me over the phone, only about ten times, that she was eighty five and a half and not as fast as she used to be! However, when no reply was forthcoming from the door I became aware of the hum of a lawnmower from around the back. I walked to the iron gates that separated the front and back garden and could see Gladys trying to push her mower through the lush new growth of grass. She wasn't really moving it, more shuffling around on the spot. I had the feeling the grass was winning, maybe even growing faster than she was cutting it!

The problem was that I couldn't get through the gates and as hard as I shouted, Gladys didn't hear. I resorted to my special weapon, an ear-piercing double-fingered power whistle that can normally wake the dead. I breathed in and let rip with the full blast. Nothing! No reaction at all. Gladys, bent over her mower, just shuffled on. Monday was not starting well, but remembering the old adage I persevered. I wasn't going to let my first call fail without a little more effort.

I looked around for something to attract her. By the front door was her plastic milk crate with one empty glass bottle. Not many people have milk delivered anymore but that plastic crate could be my saviour! I took the bottle out and practiced a few under-arm swings with it. When I thought I had it about right I let it fly. Up it went, over the iron railing, sailing through the air. To my amazement, more luck than any expertise, the milk crate landed a few feet to the left of Gladys. Nothing happened. She just kept on mowing! Suddenly she looked up at the crate and just stared at it for an age. The mower stopped. Praise the Lord I thought. I quickly shouted. Gladys looked around. "Oh Alex, I'm so sorry. I had you in my diary but forgot all about it. Hang on a shake I'll be in. Her 'shake' took a good five minutes, but eventually the front door opened. At last I could get down to work.

I watched Gladys go back out and heard the lawn mower spark up. About half an hour later I saw her manhandling it into her garden shed. She hadn't cut the grass, she had just given up! Suddenly there was a huge crash. Before I could get to the back door Gladys came stumbling in, rubbing her white hair. "Dropped a bleedin' tin of Dulux on my head. Luckily it was only a small can. My consultant told me that my bonce is so thick it could survive a nuclear blast! I think it was a compliment but I was never sure!"
"Well, you take it easy, Gladys." I said as I helped her inside and sat her at the kitchen table. "Now if you need me just call. I'll get back to the machine."

"I was coming in to make your tea, the gardener's coming next week anyway. I was just trying to help," she mumbled, rubbing her head. Her hair was now sticking up all over the place like a rag doll on drugs!

Sometime later, as I was well into fixing her old Brother VX910, Gladys came in with my cup of tea. She was back to her smiling self with neatly brushed hair. In the cup the teabag was still floating. "How dark do you like it?"

"Any shade is fine Gladys, as long as it's warm and wet." To my horror Gladys reached down with her grass-stained fingers, lifted the teabag out, squeezed it, shook the last drips back into the cup, and walked out of the room. "I'll bring the sugar and a little surprise," she threw back over her shoulder as she went. I carefully pulled a bit of grass out of the cup and sighed. I should get danger money, I thought as I heard her returning. "Now you are going to love this, Alex. A fresh baked fruit loaf made to my own recipe." Gladys plonked a spoonful of sugar in my tea, stirred it and pushed a large slice of the loaf towards me. "Looks lovely, doesn't it?"

"Gladys, that looks like perfection. Fruit loaf for breakfast suits me fine." I got stuck in to the slice, which was superb, trying not to think about what 'extra' bits of the garden might be in it!

When it was time to go, I called Gladys and told her how much my work had come to, passing her the receipt. She disappeared and returned with the sweetest smile. "I've got something very special for you. A little surprise for later!" With that, Gladys came around the back of my chair, got hold of my body-warmer, unzipped the pocket and put a roll of notes into it, all held together with a yellow elastic band. She patted me on the back, "That'll make you smile."

I drove away from my first call thinking that although it had got off to a bad start it had ended perfectly. I patted my left pocket and grinned. It looked like I was going to get a good week after all.

As I pulled into Newhaven Town Centre the traffic ground to a halt. I reached into my body-warmer pocket to see how much extra Gladys had slipped me. I pulled out the notes, slipped off the elastic band and unrolled them. It wasn't money it was the bloody recipe for her fruit loaf! I couldn't believe it. The 'old dears club' had caught me again!

I broke out into a laugh and couldn't stop. Tears were rolling down my cheeks. Those little old terrors must have some sort of underground network, passing on my details. Time and time again they catch me, and all in the most glorious ways. I glanced to my left and the group of people waiting at the bus stop were also in hysterics. They had seen me laughing and it must have triggered some sort of uncontrollable response. Slowly coming to my senses I waved and moved on.

This job, I thought, wiping away the last tear from my cheek, this job that my dad talked me into decades ago. How on earth have I ever made ends meet with those crafty old critters always getting the better of me? Still, empty pockets and a full heart, there's got to be something in that.

As I drove a thought suddenly hit me. When my Dad had uttered those immortal words to me as a kid, "Learn to love your job, Alex and you'll never work a day in your life." Maybe he already knew about the cunning old sweethearts who got everything they needed and paid for it with smiles and recipes!

Recipe for TWO Fruit Loafs (Courtesy of Gladys)

1lb of self-raising flour
4 eggs
1/4 cup of milk
1/2lb butter or marge
1/2lb sugar
1/2lb any dried or mixed fruit or nuts to suit.
Two pinches of salt and mixed spice if you like.

Mix all the ingredients in a large bowl until smooth. Grease well TWO 2lb loaf tins. Add the mix, sprinkle the top with sugar. Bake in the oven for about one hour on a medium heat. Prick with skewer. When the skewer comes out clean they are ready. Enjoy, I certainly did.

April 2019

A jay flitted across the road in front of me with a beak full of twigs. They say England, the countryside and even her mighty warships from past ages were all shaped because of our prettiest bird. They hide away autumn acorns all across the land and, unlike squirrels, who somehow remember where they hid most of their cache, the jays don't. Many of the acorns they plant sprout the following spring. As we all know, from tiny acorns huge oak trees grow. Those great oaks went on to shape the barns and buildings, ships and structures all over our green and pleasant land.

It was nearing the end of April 2019. The cherry blossom had been the best I had ever seen. For a week or more the roads and grass verges looked like they had been sprinkled with white and pink snow. A warm front had been pushed up from the continent by an obliging Jet Stream, which had also brought a dusting of reddish Saharan sand for the cars. When I had watched the forecasters announce that it was going to be warmer than Spain over the following days, I didn't believe a word of it. I mean, they always get it wrong. Don't they?

As it turned, out this Easter was going to be the hottest for 70 years! Even the Easter Bunny would need a sun hat and shades! For the past six months I had been well wrapped against everything that the elements could throw at me. In my job I could be fixing a sewing machine in a barn, factory unit, or farm, where heating would be a luxury. I was driving to work in my usual winter wear, two thin body warmers (so that I could quickly drop one if I warmed up) two pairs of socks and two jumpers. Suddenly, just like the weather forecasters had predicted, I was WAY TOO HOT. As the prickly heat crawled over my itchy skin I pulled over and began to remove layers. A passing car beeped at me as if I was doing something that was banned before the nine o'clock watershed. Wouldn't that be a sight! A fat old man doing a…no, don't even go there! Down to just a shirt and jumper I carried on in comfort.

I never know how my day is going to start, or end. I had one day last year when I came home without a penny after eight hours on the road. I've had a few days like that over the years. It's almost like gambling; you just never know. As this particular day turned out, before I got home I would be told four wonderful stories. Well, three wonderful ones and one with an old goat thrown in for good measure.

Story One

My first call brought with it an epic human tale. In the old grocers shop on the corner of Winchcombe Road in Eastbourne I was confronted by an extremely rare Singer model 44. It was an industrial treadle sewing machine, made in the great Singer factory in Kilbowie, for just a short time, in the late Victorian period. I had only seen a handful in my life. It was a cross-over from a domestic model 15 and a full size industrial model 95. It was very worn, rusty and crying out for help. As I gently turned the hand wheel I could feel that it had been well-oiled in the past and probably well-loved. All the rust was just surface rust and would be easily removed with a bit of oil and emery cloth.

It is essential with a treadle to start with the pedal and flywheel first; it should spin effortlessly. If you don't get that right the rest is a waste of time as you'll never sew well on it. Within half an hour the treadle was spinning like a toy fan in a gale. I moved up to the machine and worked away at the rust, slowly bringing the metal back to bright and shiny with fine engineering emery cloth and oil. I didn't bother with the cosmetics. I quite like a sewing machine that shows its life and age rather than just looking shiny.

As I worked I couldn't help remembering all the times as a child I would pop into the very shop I was now in. I would pick up some fruit and veg for mum or buy a banana for my lunch, which would be one penny. With 20 shillings to an old pound and 12 pennies in each shilling there would be 240 pennies to the pound. Can you imagine getting 240 bananas for a pound today!

Mrs. Baker used to run the shop. Her husband was always around for the carrying and shifting of sacks of spuds and the heavy stuff. He would also deliver groceries to the local houses. Most of the time he was outside leaning against the wall, smoking. When you walked in, the bell above the door rattled a welcome. The shop would envelop you with that wonderful smell that grocers have. Mrs. Baker was a small round woman with an easy laugh, always dressed in a hair net and cotton apron where she kept her loose change. When she needed money she used to shake her apron so that all the coins went into one corner of the front pouch, then scoop up a handful of them and, with her thick mud encrusted fingers, count aloud each one into your open hand.

I often tell (you'll have noticed by now) that it is one of the great pleasures of living in one place all your life; that each street, park, and alley holds a million memories.

While I was well under way with the Singer resurrection, Beverly recounted how her distant family fled persecution in Poland back in the 1890's. They had made their way across Europe, until boarding a boat that was heading to the shores of Britain and safety. For centuries it seems as if Britain has been the safe port in the storm for the troubles of Europe and beyond.

The family arrived homeless in Hull (now that's a title for a book). Some of the relatives immediately boarded a ship bound for America but Bev's family decided to head for London. They set up home in Whitechapel where properties were cheap after Jack the Ripper had caused so much havoc there a few years earlier.

Bev's grandfather's first task was to rent a sewing machine. Then he could start earning money at his trade as a tailor. Because of the prices of sewing machines he was unable to buy his own machine for years. It was 1899 when at last he had raised enough money to purchase the Singer 44 that I was repairing. For the next 120 years the machine stayed in the family as it was handed down, generation to generation. Oh how I wish they could talk, the stories they could tell, as they quietly witness the world turn. I managed to bring the old beast back to life, and teach Bev how to treadle. I left her with a promise to track down an instruction book and hit the road.

Story Two, The Old Goat.

You know that weird feeling that you sometimes get when you've walked into a trap? Well I was having it! The hairs on my neck were stiff and I was looking around for a quick exit. I was standing in my next customer's kitchen when I remembered that she was a moaning old goat of the first order. On my last call she had dropped her machine onto the tiled floor and it took ages to get it stitching again. I only remembered her as it was an unusual repair and she was just awful to boot.

Everything in the place was worn or damaged, there was tape around the handles of some of the pans, one of the kitchen chairs had been roughly strapped together and the table with the sewing machine on had three beer mats under one leg. Now you would be forgiven for thinking I was somewhere like an assisted dwelling or student's flat! However I was in a million pound property along one of the finest roads in town. In the drive was a top of the range Audi Q7. I had visited homes like this before. On the outside it is all show but on the inside there's an all purveying sense of meanness. Suddenly the husband who had shown me in appeared. He was bent over and moving like a whippet. "Brace yourself" he muttered, as he flew by. "DID YOU SAY SOMETHING, RAYMOND?" The wife shouted from behind me, sending me a foot into the air. "No dear, just a little cough. I'm off to the garden to weed the rhubarb like you asked." She stared at him and her fish-eyes followed him out of the room.

Then the woman started on me. "Mr Askanteruff, I've hardly used this machine since I last paid for your service. I am very disappointed in your work."
"Actually," I replied, rubbing down the hairs on my neck. "I seem to remember that I came here about ten years ago, after you knocked your machine off the table."
"Well," she hesitated. "It better not break again! I paid you nearly £40 last time and I expected more!" I could see the husband standing in the garden bent over the rhubarb. He was glancing my way under his arm. That crafty dog had scuttled off knowing exactly what was about to happen. If I hadn't remembered that last time she had tripped over the power cable on her way to open the curtains, dragging the

machine off the table, she would probably have pushed for a free repair.

God, how a handful of obnoxious customers can cut you to the quick. It's a fact that we can instantly dislike someone and she was the perfect example. Standing before me was a shrill woman in her late sixties with a pinched up face and loose straggly hair. I was in a house that must have been worth a ton and she was moaning before I had even started.

What to do? I could walk out. However in the best self-employed tradition, motivated by years struggling to make a living, I decided to go for gold. I looked at the poor Pfaff that was crying out for my help and then at the even poorer husband sheepishly weeding in the garden. I figured that I could handle her. I had become used to these odd customers that would moan about the sun coming up. I often wondered what the relatives would be thinking at their funerals!

Now, when needed, I can work fast, real fast, especially when I am in an icy environment. I decided to get to work and had the top off before she had turned the light on. I stripped down the side and carriage in a jiffy. "I'll be coming back to watch what you do so that I don't have to pay you again," she snorted as she disappeared. Not if I have anything to do with it, I thought. After she left, the husband gave me a big grin and a thumbs up from the garden. He must be some sort of saint I thought. Or maybe he liked that sort of dominatrix! The mind boggles.

I snapped out of my daydreaming and concentrated. I quickly spotted the problem. The lower drive gear had been knocked out of time and the offending needle was still jammed in the gear. I pulled it out, reset the shaft and rebuilt the machine. Decades of experience were being

brought to bear on the old Pfaff as my hands flew like the wind. The machine was sewing away as she came back in from the garden, where she had probably been telling her husband what to do (he was probably not allowed in till suppertime!). "That will be £40 please," I said, with my biggest smile as she walked in. She was quite taken aback.
"You don't hang around, do you?"
"It was easy once I had found that you had dropped a needle into the mechanism. I have also removed the needleplate damage where you have hit the plate so many times. I have removed all the fluff, which was blocking the tension assembly (I had made a nice pile of it on the table for her to see). I have also retimed your machine. You will be sewing away like a dream." She walked over and I handed her a sample of sewing that I had just done. It was stitch perfect. I saw her looking up and down each seam. I swear she almost smiled, almost!

I tell you, when you are being deliberately irritated by Lady Loathsome from Loathsome Manor, years of experience comes into play to keep everything ticking over perfectly. The end game is to get out of the house with the customer satisfied, money in my pocket, and me still sane!

My luck held. She slowed her sarcastic onslaught for a second. Probably taken aback at having to pay me twice in 10 years! It didn't last long. "I'll be paying by cheque," she announced. Leaving me in no doubt that if she was not satisfied she would cancel the cheque in an instant. Keep smiling Alex, I thought. Just keep smiling, you'll be out of here soon.

I answered all of her following questions with the most wonderful smile that could only be matched if you went on a seminar at The Acme Smiling College at Smilington-On-Sea (no that's not real, leave Google alone!).

As soon as the front door closed behind me I wanted to shout YIPEEE. If I never saw the old goat again it would be a month too soon!

As I got to my car her husband suddenly appeared from the side passage. He looked around sheepishly and came over to me with an armful of the most wonderful sticks of green and pink rhubarb. I quickly put them in my boot. "Don't let her see or she'll weigh them and charge you." He thanked me as if I had just saved his life, shook my hand and shot off. It turned out she sewed on the machine most days but since she broke it she had been helping him in the garden! Well, instructing him in the garden. With her machine working he may have got some peace and all would be well with the world once more.

Funnily, the foul calls that come along are the hardest to deal with but the most financially rewarding. I am in and out in moments and don't dilly dally along the way. When I hit a call that I enjoy I can run so late. Sometimes I even forget to ask for payment! And as you know, I often get cheated with a smile and a slice of cake. Interestingly I have just received a payment through the post from a lovely customer who I had completely forgot to charge! Yana just shrugs her shoulders and smiles. Such is life. Still the old goat was behind me and my wheels were rolling towards my next encounter.

Story Three

Spring is an amazing time of year in England. It produces a feast for the eyes. I mean even the brick walls come to life with yellow wallflowers and aubrietia, billowing out clouds of blossom, like mini purple waterfalls exploding from the walls. As I drove I relaxed. Nearly 20 minutes early, I knocked on my next customer's door. Another great tale was about to unfold.

I found myself sitting opposite a sweet, wide-faced, smiley old girl with enormous hearing aids and a pair of diamond encrusted glasses. She had a fine fluff of hair over her face like an old bear. Somehow we got to talking about what she did during the Second World War. I had guessed from her age that she may have been too young to join the armed forces but old enough to work in some capacity. I was spot on. I took a big slurp of my coffee and carried on oiling her Singer model 306k as she rambled away.

"The war had started and land was desperately needed to grow food," my customer said as she chatted. "We developed land in South London out of old building plots and allotments then ploughed it over. We fertilised it with rotten fish and bone meal from the local abattoir. We then used it for intensive farming for the next six years. We grew everything from carrots to cabbages as fast as we could, all to feed the ever-hungry Capital. War might have been going on but we all still needed to eat!"

"We saw a few Doodle Bugs. 'Orrible little critters they were. They made the most awful noise to let you know they were coming. We would all look up and shout out "DOODLE BUG, DOODLE BUG, DOODLE OFF AND DON'T COME BACK! Every now and again we would see Spitfires chasing them, trying to turn them around. By tipping the bugs wings with their own plane's wings they could sometimes change the bomb's direction. Crazy but valiant. We never had a direct hit on us but they came close. Several times, when one went off near us, officials would turn up and collect any scraps they could find from the bomb. After taking photos they would pack it all away, each piece carefully labelled. Then they would all disappear as quickly as they had arrived. We never did find out what they were after. Information I suppose!"

"It was mainly women on the farm but there were a few men working there. Farming was a reserved occupation. It meant if you were farming you didn't get enlisted in the armed forces, not to start with anyway. Later on there were even a few prisoners of war for a while. We also had two pacifists who refused to fight but helped in every other way. After the war ended the authorities built enormous high rise flats on our ground and it looked like our little farm never existed. Strange times, those."

As I left the 306k was purring like a new-born kitten. My mind was a blur thinking about those crazy young fighter pilots chasing bombs in the sky. I looked down at my notes. I had just one more call to an old customer who I had seen many times. She would tell me one of the strangest stories of all and well worth putting down in print. I may not have remembered it exactly, but here is the core of it, and it is amazing. The tales I pick up while fixing sewing machines always astonish me. You know I could almost write a book. Or ten!

Story Four

My final story of the day was a gem of a tale. My customer's brother had arrived to help put in and set up an aquarium in their little London flat. This was way back in the 1960's and the dismal inner city flats could be brightened up with all sorts of furnishings. While they were putting it up, the brother's watch slipped from his wrist and dropped behind the tank. No one noticed until he was about to leave. They realised they would have to drain the tank to move it to get the watch back. Her brother just laughed and told her he was given it on set while filming anyway. It didn't cost him a penny so if she ever found it she could keep it.

Well they never moved and the tank stayed put, as did the watch. Eventually as the years rolled by, the couple decided to move out of London and retire down to my area (and bring me this great story). Low and behold after they had drained the tank and moved it there was the watch sitting on the floor, covered in dust. The brother had long since died and it was a lovely reminder of him, especially as everyone had forgotten all about it. After they moved down here they took the watch into Bruford's in Cornfield Road, Eastbourne, to see if it could be cleaned and repaired.

Bruford's informed them that it was a fake Rolex, the makers had not even bothered to copy the dial correctly. It was hardly worth the cost of a service, but it was up to them. Because it had belonged to her brother and had sentimental value, they decided to have it serviced anyway, just as a little keepsake from happier times. Her brother had been a stunt man and always loved 'showy' watches. When they used to meet up he would delight her with stories from famous film sets and other fabulous tales.

A few weeks later Bruford's rang to tell them that the man who serviced it was surprised at the quality of the mechanism. When he checked the Rolex serial numbers it was not on their lists. However for £50 he could send it to Switzerland to see if they could track it down. Now, my customer had already had to pay for the service and another £50 was a bit much, so they told them not to bother. However the next day they changed their minds and the watch was packed off to Rolex in Switzerland.

Weeks went by when the phone rang. It was the manager of Bruford's. Now this is the amazing bit. The watch that had been sitting behind their aquarium for nearly 40 years was one of only six watches made for one of the first James Bond films. Even more, Rolex would like to purchase it back! Amazingly the money they offered was enough to pay off all their loans and buy a new car! Now that is what you call a nice surprise!

Funny how life is, they had struggled for years and sitting right next to them all the time was a watch worth many times its weight in gold! Told you it was a cracker.

The Singer model 44 looks quite ordinary but in fact it is one of the rarest of all Singer industrial machines. It is an ugly beast, made between 1890-1900. It was a cross between and industrial and a domestic model 15. The machine was so basic that it did not even have a reverse but still cost the equivalent of a year's wage! The machine may be ugly but it is a phenomenal sewer, handling everything from silk to leather. Of course it can only go as fast as your legs can pedal! Strangely the angle poise sewing lamp is worth more than the machine today.

My friends tell me that as I get older I'm starting to look more like a wide mouth frog! I have no idea what they're on about...

Lilacs & Lilies

Ancient folklore tells that if you wash your face in the early dew, as the mayflower blossoms, on the first day of May, you will have a fair complexion all year. Sounds great but you have to do it before the sun rises. At this time of year that is around 5.00am! May Day has many tales and traditions from twirling around the Maypole to Morris Dancers strapped with bells bouncing up the high street. I suppose it's the sudden warmth, the blood is up after a lazy winter and the British start to do their crazy stuff!

I decided against leaping out of bed and having a facial in the cold grass as dawn broke. At my age no one was going to notice my complexion. Hey, I might even enjoy a teenage spot or two! There was also another reason I wasn't moving like a greyhound from a gypsy camp. A few days earlier I had done something so stupid that it even took me by surprise!

My wheelie bin was stuffed to the brim with cardboard and I needed to dispose of another box. Easy-peasy. With my vastly superior intelligence I dragged the bin to my plastic garden chair. Are the bells ringing yet? It would have been far easier to bring the chair to the bin! I then climbed from the chair into the bin and started to bounce up and down. Well, as much as a large old man can bounce up and down. Usually my weight has the desired effect on the bin and the cardboard gets pushed down. However this was not 'the usual'. As I majestically bounced up and down like a leaping gazelle, I started to enjoy myself. For a second or two my distant youth returned. It did not last! Suddenly the bin (which was on a slope) decided to follow the laws of gravity and flew away to the left. I came down with all my might as it disappeared from under me. One second I was flying with the garden birds, the next I face-planted the block paving in the front garden. CRUNCH!

It gets worse! The previous weeks I had been suffering from a nasty cold and it had messed with my balance. Being thrown on the floor was bad enough but then the world started spinning. I was like a drunk after a bar fight, clinging to the foot of his barstool. Suddenly, Yana appeared. She helped me up with a few choice words and dragged me inside to patch me up. Amazingly, once again, I was badly bruised but not broken. The result was that over the following days I had pains in places I didn't know existed and I limped everywhere. Stairs were a nightmare, but it gave my customers a few giggles!

All my calls were slow and steady and with each pain I swore I would never crush waste in a wheelie bin again. Would I stick to it though? The older I get the more stupid things I seem to do. I used to be amazed when I turned up at my customers and found them clinging onto apple trees, pruning the branches, or half way up their chimney stacks altering their television antennas in their pyjamas. Now I seem to be the idiot who is doing the same stuff!

My first customer of the day was also one of my oldest ones. J E Smiths, along Langney Road, are Eastbourne's longest established upholstery business. They are experts in re-upholstery. The first family member of the Smiths, George Smith, had arrived in Eastbourne in 1860. He was an artilleryman, based at the Redoubt Fortress on the seafront. The Redoubt was originally built to supply the smaller Martello Forts along the coast during the Napoleonic Wars. By 1860 it was still being maintained as a fighting fort in case of invasion, but in a far less rigorous manner. While stationed in Eastbourne, George might not have had to fight off invaders but he found the time to have, and bring up, ten children!

James Smith set up and ran Eastbourne's longest established upholstery business. His grandsons run the business today.

One of his kids, James Ernest Smith, set up as an upholsterer in 1918, just after World War One. His son Albert took over after he retired. I used to fix Albert's old machines when he needed. When he gave up he phoned and asked me about the latest upholstery machines. At the time he was doing a lot of high quality hotel work. I suggested the Brother B791, a superb industrial sewing machine with a needle feed that eliminated puckering. He ordered the machine and all the extra feet to go with it. It was a leaving present for his two sons, Gary and, Jim so that they could carry on the family's good work.

I was now working for his sons who are the fourth generation of Smiths from the Redoubt. It was a great call as I was not working on one of the normal huge industrials, but a small domestic Singer 17k hand crank, which had been made up in Kilbowie in 1903. Their grandfather had ordered it but for some unknown reason it ended up in the Post Office at East Dean, four miles away from where he lived in Eastbourne. That didn't put James off. When he received a note saying that it was there, he walked over the hills and returned that night carrying the machine! Now, even the domestic Singers weigh the same as a baby elephant, so that was some feat. I suppose in those days there was little alternative. I spent an hour in the workshop listening to the story of the old Singer while I was bringing it back to life. I was soon back on the road, heading off to my next customer.

I had not expected to be working on this small and beautiful Singer when I called at J E Smith's Upholstery. Normally I am working on long arm industrial machines that you can almost climb through with needles like nails.

At my next customers I was caught on my knees sniffing some lily of the valley, "They're lovely aren't they Alex!"
"Lilacs and lilies, my two favourite spring flowers, Julie." I answered, as I staggered to my feet.
"Well, I'll pick a bunch for you before you leave. With 28 grandchildren they will all be gone by the weekend! Charlie is looking forward to seeing you. He wanted to know if you have been practicing your French polishing?"

"Not half. I have almost perfected it. His tip of flicking the oil over the polish before using the 'rubber' was worth its weight in gold. It has transformed my polishing on the old sewing machine cases."

Charlie had spent his life in the London furniture trade. After a five year apprenticeship he went to work for a large furniture makers and spent 45 years perfecting his art. When he retired down to Eastbourne (and met me) he took the time to pass on his knowledge of how to get a really good shine on wood. Not as easy as people think. In fact it was almost impossible for me until I bumped into Charlie while I was fixing his wife's machine. He taught me the 'loading' of the rubber (a wad of padded cotton soaked in polish), the mixing of shellac polish, the complex hand movements along the grain of the wood, and finally the secret of linseed oil for perfecting the shine. Each time I brought an old wooden box back to life I thought of Charlie. Most important of all, he taught me patience, the secret of great French Polishing.

As I walked up the twitten to The Pumpkin Patch in Hailsham, my next call, I was confronted with a big chalkboard sticking out into the alley. The board screamed in huge white words, 'FANCY THE BEST BOOBS IN TOWN!' I didn't know where to look, I almost blushed. Next to my haberdashery, a new cosmetic surgery shop had opened. As I went in to The Pumpkin Patch the girls were giggling. Joe sparked up, "We saw you reading the sign, Alex."
"Well, you can't exactly miss it, can you!"
"Are you thinking about it then?" One of the girls giggled.
"Leave me alone. You lot are going to be the death of me. Mind you, I could get a nice new pair and then a big tattoo from that tattoo parlour up the road! Hasn't Hailsham changed from the old market town it used to be?"

"You have to roll with the times, Alex. Our local shops have to transform or die. As much as Amazon and all those on-line shops can do, they can't supply tattoos or boobs by post!"

"Right," I coughed, "I think I'll let you girls carry on. I'll get upstairs and sort out the sewing machines." I could hear them laughing as I climbed the stairs. Whatever people tell you, when a bunch of girls get together they can tease a man rotten. And you know who the worst ones are? Nuns. Yes, hard to believe I know, but you get a handful of nuns together, especially on their own turf, and they can give you hell.

Before long I was rolling up Featherbed Lane towards Cowbeech and my next call. I was off to see Maureen and she had a lovely surprise waiting for me. The car smelt like heaven as I drove. The scent of Lily of the Valley had filled the Suzuki with the sweetest perfume, mingling with the fresh spring air from the fields. The banks and hedgerows were a multi-coloured quilt of yellows, blues and greens as cowslips and bluebells blended in with the fresh grass. The first day of May was as perfect a day as Mother Nature could ever create.

I pulled up at Maureen's right underneath the most wonderful light blue Lilac tree in full bloom. Cowbeech is one of those villages in my area that has been bypassed by time. An old inhabitant from a century back would recognise the place in a heartbeat. One main street with a pub at the end, the odd road or two splitting off into rolling countryside. It is a patch of heaven. It has become a rat run at peak times but besides that, pretty much the perfect place to retire.

As I got out of the car there was a little thud on the roof. I turned to see a chubby bumble bee completely covered in pollen, upside down on the car roof. Its back legs looked like they had orange rucksacks on. It must have just fallen out of the tree above. I was transfixed as the little bug wriggled around on its back for a while before stretching out its legs and righting itself. It rubbed its eyes with its front legs, shook its wings, turned in a circle, and made a very heavy take-off. It noisily buzzed away like a drunken teenager, straight back up to the lilac tree for more nectar and pollen. I thought that if the honey bees were doing as well as that fat little bumble bee, then it's going to be a good year for the honey sellers.

Maureen was on her knees trimming up her garden with an old pair of red shears. "Spot on time again, Alex. I could set the church clock to your arrivals."
"No, don't Maureen. These days it's hit and miss if I make it or not. Some days I can run so far behind I think a horse and cart might be faster."
"Well today you're bang on time. You know, I was looking back at my old receipts that I've kept with my machine. The first time you called on me was back in the eighties, over 30 years ago."
"And we're both still here! Amazing," I laughed back. "I was a young lad full of energy and jet black hair. Now I want to fall asleep at any time past seven and fancy an afternoon nap most days. Oh, and don't get me started on my old grey bonce."
"Well at least you have hair. My Cyril went as bald as a coot after our first child was born. I don't think he could handle the sleepless nights. Now, you hold onto these shears and help me up so that I can put the kettle on."

Inside her pretty little cottage, the wood burner was still chugging away, giving the place a smell like an over-smoked kipper. I never understood the appeal of these terrible polluters of our modern age. Yes, an open fire looks lovely, but there are so many cleaner alternatives now that give the appearance without the poison. A customer of mine explained that we are fighting tradition. Humans have had fires forever, so it would be a hard thing to break them of it. Tradition is a good excuse for many things. I wonder how the Vikings broke their tradition of 'burn and pillage'. Someone must have made them understand that what 'they' enjoy may not be so good for others! As I watched the last embers of the fire crackle away I knew I was witnessing the end of a way of life. With over a thousand people a week dying directly from air pollution in this country, the days of unfiltered open fires were limited.

I got down to work on a beautifully preserved electric Singer model 99, probably the most common older sewing machine that I come across. I had just been filming a documentary for the BBC on the massive Singer factory in Scotland. It was called The Singer Story, Made in Clydebank. Its rise and fall was spectacular and the tales from the workers were poignant. At one point several of them started crying when they talked about how much fun it was to work there, and how sad it was to see the huge factory being pulled down. A way of life for generations suddenly gone forever. In this book is the story End of Empire, written about the great northern powerhouse that dominated Kilbowie and Clydebank.

What caught me most was watching the women sew on the 99. These were true professionals that knew the machine backwards. They would start by spinning the chrome spoked hand wheel, then carry on turning the wooden hand-crank itself, as fast as they could. Then, with the machine spinning like a top, they would guide the work through. At the end of a seam they would 'palm' down the spinning chrome hand wheel to a perfect halt. They could sew as fast as any electric: I had never seen anything like it. Their mastery of these old hand machines was a joy to watch. When I tried it I jammed my machine within six inches!

As I was working away, Maureen appeared, clutching her massive old tailor's scissors. I had always drooled over her professional Wilkinson Sheffield shears. They were 13 inches long, hollow ground hardened steel and weighed a ton. However, once you slid them on they somehow became weightless. They would slice through a lump of heavy denim or a single thread from a spider's web. I used to love the 'swishing' sound they made as they sliced fabric. I knew she had paid a fortune for them and I was in for the biggest surprise of the day.

"I haven't used these since you were last here, Alex. I was wondering if you might like to take them off my hands. Do you remember me telling you about how I got them?"
"It was a shop in Bexhill wasn't it?" I excitedly replied.
"Well I never. You must have been listening. Fancy remembering that! Yes it was Gowers the dressmakers, along Devonshire Road in Bexhill-on-Sea. I started my apprenticeship there at fifteen, just a week after leaving school. Mr Rosenberg who ran the shop was a dragon, and pay was low. I made it through the first week with plenty of tears. By the third week Mr Rosenberg actually smiled at me. By the end of the month I was skipping to work. Then came a bombshell. I was so looking forward to my first ever payday. In my mind I had spent it twice over. Mr Rosenberg had other ideas. He presented me with these actual shears. With great gravity he explained that they were the finest shears money could buy and used by none other than the Queen's dressmaker, Norman Hartnell, and many Savile Row tailors. He explained that he had been watching me most carefully. He knew that I would probably spend a lifetime in the sewing trade, so he had put

in a special order to Wilkinson in Sheffield. He presented me with these scissors and I blushed with pride.

I was the happiest girl in the world until I went up to the office that Friday for my pay. I was told the scissors cost 23shillings and 6 pence and were deducted from my wages. I was handed a pay packet with six bob in it for the month! That didn't even cover my bus fare! The crafty old sod. Mind you he was a wonderful dressmaker and could cut a perfect pattern out in a flash. I eventually forgave him and 56 years later I still have these scissors. If only I could lift them with one hand! Still I would love you to have them, Alex. I know you will cherish them." With that Maureen handed me the shears with her shaky little hands. I felt like a knight being handed the finest blade in the kingdom.

"Oh Maureen, you've made my day. No, my week. No, my whole year. You know I've always drooled over these. I've never come across a pair of shears that cut like they do and feel so beautifully balanced. They are like a great sword made by the finest bladesmiths in the land. I will treasure them always."

"Well they are yours to look after now." I smiled and gave her the biggest hug. When I left I waved and shouted, "See you in another 30 years." She laughed back, "If I phoned you in 30 years we would both be in for a shock!"

As I drove away smiling, a memory suddenly sprung to mind from one of my old 'teasing nuns'. She had been listening to me moaning about all my aches and pains as I fixed her convent machines. She came out with one of the best one-liners ever. "Alex, old age is no place for the weak. Buck up, toughen up, and remember, no one gets out alive!"

That night I was deep in meditation, well my form of meditation, which involves watching gardening on television with a cup of tea and some McVitie's Rich Tea biscuits. I kept glancing at Maureen's scissors, which were shining temptingly at me from the oak dresser. You know the old saying, don't give a builder a hammer, he just starts looking for a nail! Well I am the same with scissors. I had cut just about everything that could be cut. I had been told in so uncertain terms to put them down before they got banned from the house! Suddenly I remembered that I had unplugged Maureen's freezer when I used the socket for her sewing machine. I rushed to the phone and rang her. "Maureen," I gasped, "I forgot to plug your freezer back in!"

"You silly sausage, Alex. I did it as soon as you left. See you in 30 years!" The phone went dead in my hand. I hung up, laughed, shook my head and went back to my meditating. I glanced admiringly at the scissors but proudly walked by without even touching them. Such control!

I adore professional scissors. A good pair would have once cost a week's wage. Did you know that you can always tell a nice pair of scissors? If you hold them up to the light, closed, you should be able to see a gap between the blades. This is because good blades only touch along their length at the place the blades pass each other. This gives a clean, smooth cut and, if you listen closely, a beautiful 'swishing' sound.

Emergency Services

There are many emergency services: the main ones of course, which can mean life or death, but also dozens of minor ones from locksmiths to plumbers. Breakdowns of all sorts all over the planet, repaired by a world of specialists. I am one of those 'extra' emergency services, the one for women in sewing peril. I am called to divert a last minute catastrophe, from the half made prom dress to the school sewing exam or a similar problem. Anything from tulle skirts for the Royal Ballet to Glyndebourne Opera costumes. The phone starts squawking at first light and can sometimes carry on until bats are flying around the belfry.

Derek, the tailor from Cole's in Uckfield was the first on my list. Established in 1928, Cole's Menswear are one of the few survivors in the high street. There was a time when Cole's three-piece suits were not worn by the 'hoi polloi' but bank managers, millionaires and wealthy landowners. For how long the 'cutters of distinction' (now in their third generation) can continue is anyone's guess as competition from online retailers gets ever stronger. A stone's throw along the High Street is my other favourite shop in Uckfield, which is even older, Carvills. They often win awards for their shop, which looks like it has somehow escaped from Knightsbridge in London. It is always a great pleasure to get a call from the family firm when one of their soft furnishing machines is kaput. I have been known to spend as much time wandering around the shop as fixing their machines!

Surprisingly, Derek, back at Cole's, does not use an industrial for his sewing but a Singer 201K domestic set into a flat table. The machine, made in the 1950's, has been so used that the black enamel has worn away, leaving just the polished aluminium bed of the machine. She is beautifully worn, well-oiled and well maintained. She makes the most wonderful sound as she sews. The shop is stuffed full of expensive menswear from Hugo James to Barbour. They also make their living from hiring out wedding suits and all the paraphernalia that goes along with those special days.

The rain was coming down in a heavy, lazy way as I left Cole's. I swung my back pack on, pulled my collar up and slipped down the back alleys to my car, which was parked in Tesco's car park. I jumped in and headed for Heathfield along the Buxted Road. As I drew near to Heathfield High Street I glanced over to my left. I used to love calling on an old customer down a little drive. I swear Dick King Smith must have based his book called The Sheep-Pig about Babe after seeing their home. Chickens and geese used to run around the grounds. Well, the chickens used to run around. The geese were quite happy to sit on the gravel drive and block it, nosily objecting when I tried to drive down it. The hubby would always be pottering around the garden. I'll tell you something funny. He had the biggest earlobes I had ever seen, like pink spoons glued to the side of his head, plus there was always a ponderous drip of snot swinging from the tip of his huge nose. When I talked to him I found it hard to concentrate. I would be transfixed by his flapping ears and his whopping conk. Strangely, as much as that hypnotic snot swung like a pendulum, it never fell! He also had made a magical gate that opened with the softest touch of the latch. It would slowly swing (via several pulleys and weights) until it clicked fully open. When you touched the latch at the other end it would close just the same. It was a perfect piece of 'bodged' engineering; my favourite kind! It was all gone now. A new estate of plush properties with no gardens had appeared where their lovely old dilapidated house once hid, half obscured by the woods around it. All that are left of that couple and their house now are my memories.

I arrived at my next customer's with all hell breaking loose. Three teenage daughters were having tantrums as they prepared for school and the noise was ear-piercing. Everyone was shouting at everyone as I was directed to the sewing machine. Luckily I can quickly become invisible. I just put my head down and get to work. Within moments I become no more interesting than a vase on the mantelpiece.

The mum looked ragged, her brown hair all twisted and tangled, spiking upwards in places as if she was full of static electricity. One of the kids was shouting at the top of her voice because her mum had told her to remove her nail varnish before she left for school. Apparently her teacher would go bananas if it was spotted. Another was messily scooping up cornflakes as if her life depended on it. Beneath her was a large white fluffy dog eagerly catching the flakes and drips as they fell. Another dog had come and sat quietly by my side, looking lovingly up at me. Someone had obviously stolen one of the other girl's phones because it wasn't where she had left it in her bag! Suddenly a sister appeared in the doorway and nearly threw it at her, telling her she had left it in the bathroom. Oh it gets worse…!

Suddenly the mother screamed. The family cat had snapped and made a dash for freedom across the sideboard, knocking over the nail varnish remover on the mum's new white maple sideboard. It was obviously the last straw. The mum was shouting at her daughter as she desperately scrubbed the sideboard. I now had two dogs under the table at my feet, and a terrified ginger cat. The mum then shouted at me as if I was the husband she was obviously divorcing! I needed to move my car as it was blocking the drive. As I got up I noticed the cat had peed on the hardwood floor by my feet. I said nothing but obediently moved my car. She sped out of the drive with the three kids still shouting at each other. The car looked like hell on wheels as it raced by. I just shook my head. Over the years I had seen it all before. I once called on a house with 11 kids! I'm sure that's in one of my older books.

I closed the driveway gates and walked back towards the house. Both the dogs came out to greet me and I ushered them inside. All of a sudden the house was stunningly quiet. The hush was so thick you could almost hug it. The old house seemed to breathe a quiet sigh and then the large grandfather clock in the hall chimed a mellow nine. I found some kitchen roll, wiped up the cat pee and then got back to work.

By the time my customer came home she was looking ten years younger, even her hair had calmed down! The drive home on her own must have done her good. She fed her dogs, stroked the cat, and made a cup of coffee. She shook her head at the stain on her new sideboard and came over to me. She sat down, took a sip of the coffee, which she was cradling, looked up at me, and for the first time, smiled. I was surprised how pretty she was. I had only seen the dragon and now the princess had appeared.

"It happens every day," she sighed. I'm sure if they showed us a film clip of teenagers we would never have started a family!"

"I've seen worse. At least a million times," I smiled back. "Believe me you get payback when you're older. The good news is that your machine is sewing like new. At least that's one problem out of the way." As I left, my customer was standing in the doorway sipping her coffee. The dogs were on either side of her and even the cat looked relaxed!

****

Sometimes I think I know what Marco Polo felt like when he wandered off around the world. I am thrown crazy instructions over the phone, "I was given your name by my friend. Could you call to fix my machine?"
"Yes of course. Where do you live?"
"Opposite her, silly!" I then spend ages trying to narrow down which town and street. Often, when my customers are deep in the Sussex countryside I am told things like, "Count the number of telephone poles. We are nine from the main road." I was once told to count 32 white painted blocks from Newick Village Green. "Can't miss it," she threw in at the end of her ridiculous instructions! If I had a penny for every time someone in the country told me there was a green hedge nearby I would be a millionaire! Sometimes, when I do eventually find my customer, the first words I fancy spouting are, "Doctor Livingstone I presume?"

****

The morning passed with all my usual calls and lunchtime was soon looming. As I drove the clouds suddenly split and puffed up into great billowing balls. Rays of sun burst through onto the wet road and my grey world instantly exploded into full colour. The sky unexpectedly seemed to be full of huge grey-bottomed galleons with billowing yellow sails, set for the distant horizon where some great battle in the sky would take place. God, the British weather is a wonderful thing. Except for high summer or midwinter there are hardly ever two days the same.

Along the country roads, tables selling goods had started to appear. They always start around summertime; eggs, jams, bunches of flowers. By Autumn it would be apples, chutneys, pumpkins and countless other produce. If I see honey or ducks eggs I usually screech to a halt and grab some.

My next customer of the day was a beauty. Her grandson had heard her talking about the old hand sewing machine that she once had so many times, that one evening he bid for one on Ebay, and won. The only problem was that he was bidding through 'beer goggles' and was nine cans of Heineken the worse for wear. He ended up paying seventy quid for a machine that was 'sold as seen'. When it arrived they couldn't even get the lid off, so I was called.

Sitting on a lovely old table was a domed wooden Singer case waiting for me to operate. My customer, a sweet old girl, just 86 years young, was apprehensive. "Please call me Ava. You don't mind if I call you Alex, do you? So many villagers around here recommended you, I feel as if I know you already."
"You call me what you like, Ava. No one can pronounce my surname. Alex is fine."
"Well Alex, I don't even know if I can sew anymore. It's been years. I wish I never went on to Albert so much about all the things I used to make. He is a dear, and full of good intentions but, well, how can I say it without sounding cruel, when he's bored and has been drinking he's a little devil."
"I'm sorry." I said (I had laughed out loud). I didn't mean to be rude, it's just that we all do silly things, don't we."

"Oh I suppose so, but he is nearly thirty now so he should know better. He's living with me while he settles into his new job. If he likes it and stays he will get a place of his own. Don't tell him but I do so enjoy his company. If he does move out I'll miss him dreadfully. I have been so lonely since my dear Al died. He is even named after him too."

Suddenly the room was full of emotion and Ava started to choke back tears. I had learnt from experience to quickly move the topic of conversation on, especially when departed husbands roll into them. "What's that wonderful smell, Ava?"
"Lunch! Fried eggs, bacon and fried beans. I fry the beans in the bacon fat. I have made way too much as usual. Would you like to join me?" A sudden vision of the dry ham sandwich warming in my car jumped into my mind. "Wow Ava, I am famished. That smell would drive a priest to sin. I would love some."

Instead of fixing a sewing machine I suddenly found myself sitting at the kitchen table tucking into a feast, washed down with sweet tea. Slightly better than my warm sandwich I thought to myself with a smile.

"You have just gobbled that up like an escaped prisoner's first meal, Alex. I see you don't get it at home."
"I've never had beans fried in bacon fat in my life, Ava. It's amazing. For God's sake don't tell my wife."
"Well, whatever she is feeding you Alex, you look very well on it!" Ava replied suspiciously, running a beady eye over my rotund figure.
"Oh I have supply lines stretched across Sussex, Ava. Thousands of customers willing to feed their starving soldier when I arrive to do battle with their machines. Anyway, I thought this food is supposed to kill you?" I

added enthusiastically while pushing a piece of toast around the plate to mop up the beans.

"Don't be daft. I'll tell you what will kill you. Processed food. They should rename it 'poison food'. So called 'experts' tell you don't eat meat, don't eat eggs, and don't eat butter and all the rest. They don't stand back and ask why the people who grew up on that stuff are now the oldest generation that has ever lived? The experts went a bit quiet for a while when they found out the oldest woman on the planet was eating several eggs a day!"

"Interestingly all the rumours, and what I call propaganda, started at about the same time as processed foods came on so strong in the supermarkets. There were no supermarkets when I was growing up. The closest thing we got to preserved food was tin cans. I'm not saying there is a connection but we grew up on meat and two veg, good clean simple stuff. They tell us don't drink milk, don't do this or that. Most of the old-fashioned simple foods have now been replaced with highly processed foods with a million additives, colourings and 'E' numbers. Do you know they even grow potatoes in fluids now to speed up production? Potatoes at the bottom and tomatoes growing up the strings above, no soil in sight. No wonder they are tasteless. Millions of years of evolution replaced with a scientific concoction. They call it Hydroponics and I hate it. Clean water and good food is so important to a growing child."

"There are so many young people suffering from such horrible allergies and diseases now. Do you know that cancer will touch one out of every two people today! When I was a child you hardly ever heard the word. It would be whispered about a great aunt or a friend of a friend. Now it is like a plague on humans and it all started around the same time as heavily processed foods. I may be no expert but I look a lot healthier than my doctor. I do worry about him so!"

Ava probably had a point. I had heard it more than once from these tough old women who seem to outlive everyone. I wasn't totally convinced and I was no food specialist but she did look amazing for her age. "Time I got to the machine," I announced with a satisfied rubbing of my belly.

After some careful wriggling with screwdrivers there was a click and the lid lifted a fraction. I removed it to reveal a stunning Singer model 17 hand machine, made around 1910. The decals were superb and the whole machine had a layer of dust, showing it had not been touched for years. "I think this is going to come up great. Is that the kettle I hear?"
"What do you fancy?"
"Coffee, milk, two sugars please." Ava went off to make my drink and I got down to work. The winder rubber had gone solid and needed prising off and replacing. The long boat shuttle was locked into the machine but soon came out with some oil and gentle persuasion. Drops of oil were fed into all the holes and the machine was slowly brought back to life. As I worked I drank coffee and listened to Ava's life. In the garden the first swallows of the year were flitting across her perfect lawn, feeding up on insects before nesting. They had timed their flight from Africa to perfectly coincide with the new crop of bugs in our Sussex countryside. Her garden was immaculate and I asked her how she did it. It turned out that her grandson, Albert, helped with the garden. Although he was a computer programmer there was nothing he enjoyed more than digging out flowerbeds and planting things. "He has natural green fingers my dear Albert. Who would guess when he

has spent most of his life playing on computers? He just loves the outdoors."

Once the machine was perfect I downloaded a new instruction book from her computer (which was way faster than mine), and printed it out for her. We went through the machine together as years rolled away. "I remember making my first christening gown, oh, and Mary's bridesmaid's dress. It's all coming back now. Well, Alex. Be honest. Did Albert pay too much?"
"Actually your grandson has got the deal of the month. This machine has been rocketing up in value recently. Especially in the condition this beauty is in. It would not surprise me if this machine won't be worth hundreds in a few years. I mean, where have you ever seen anything of this quality? It's a stunner, not just for now, but for all time. And look how well it fits into your beautiful cottage. Your grandson has done you proud. And who would have guessed you also learnt on a shuttle machine. That is so lucky, or maybe fate!"
We carried on sewing. I glanced down at my watch. I had been there way too long. I was packing up my tools when I heard the garden gate and looked out of the cottage window. Backing in the gate was a tall deliveryman. He was about six-four and carrying three bags of compost! One under his left arm and two more on his right shoulder. As he turned I was immediately reminded of that superb Hollywood actor Rock Hudson. The deliveryman seemed to have jumped straight out of the pages of a Mills & Boon romantic novel, dressed in light blue jeans with a loose fitting but brightly coloured short-sleeved shirt, splattered with small yellow flowers (they turned out to be ducks), over a tight white T-shirt. He had jet black curly hair, shining in the sun, and designer stubble, outlining a masculine jaw.

"Ava, Ava," I shouted. "Come and look at this. It will make you smile for a week. You have the best looking deliveryman on Planet Earth coming up your path. He's just bringing in a truck load of compost in one go!" Ava toddled over to me and looked out of the window as 'Rock' put the bags down by the side of the lawn. He leant forward and straighten the bags into a neat pile before brushing off his denims. He turned to us staring at him and waved, backing it up with a million dollar smile. "That's no delivery man. That's my grandson Albert! He's the one responsible for you being here today, the one who bought the sewing machine. He is a wonder, isn't he!"

"Well," I coughed a little, "I'm lost for words."

"If you're lost for words, can you imagine what happens when I go into town with him? I sometimes go shopping just for a giggle, to watch people walking into lamp posts and benches as he strolls along. The way he distracts people he should come with a health warning! ALBERT, ALBERT," she shouted, waving like mad, "COME AND SAY HELLO."

Funny isn't it, I had all the wrong first impressions of Ava's 'little devil'. I had assumed that Albert would be a quiet spotty geek, tapping away on a computer keyboard in a stuffy office somewhere, programing cash machines or that sort of thing. In reality he was a movie star that delivered granny's compost! When he managed to squeeze into the cottage he was delighted to hear that he had not bought a 'pup' for his gran. Ava proudly gave him a demonstration on the Singer. I left with her promising to make him something for Christmas. I'm not sure how pleased he would be but I knew, looking like he did, even a bin liner would look great on him!

The afternoon flew by but I had one more brilliant surprise in store before Father Time nicked another day from me. I was home cleaning up, scrubbing the grease from under my nails, bent over the kitchen sink while staring aimlessly out of the window, when someone vaguely familiar walked in the gate, struggling with a sewing machine. I shouted to Yana that he looked like an older version of my engineering teacher back at college. I knew it wasn't as I hadn't set eyes on him since I was nineteen, 43 years ago, and he would be long dead. How wrong I was. "Oh, actually it is! It's Mr Beaumont. He phoned earlier. I said you would be back by six. He has a problem with his wife's sewing machine. As hard as he has tried, he just can't fix it!"

"Well, well well," I said with the biggest smile. "If that isn't poetic justice. The master needs his student's help! How the world turns." I grabbed a towel to dry my hands and ran to the door. This was going to be a delight!

Herstmonceux Castle looks like something out of a 1950's Hollywood movie. Set in private woodlands it is a joy to visit. You can also fly birds of prey around the estate. Here I am with Cruz the vulture. Amazingly vultures are endangered as their natural habitat disappears. Cruz seems quite at home in the Sussex countryside though.

Did you know that East Sussex has more ancient flint churches than anywhere on earth? Here is the wonderful Grade 1 listed St Andrews Church in Alfriston and the stunning Simon and St Jude in East Dean. Whatever your beliefs, sitting in peaceful ancient monuments like these soothes the soul.

Besides Isaac Singer and Elias Howe, Allen B Wilson was the most important sewing machine pioneer in the 19th Century. His inventions are still used on sewing machines today. This wonderful image of Wilson was recently uncovered by his relative Helen DeFoe.

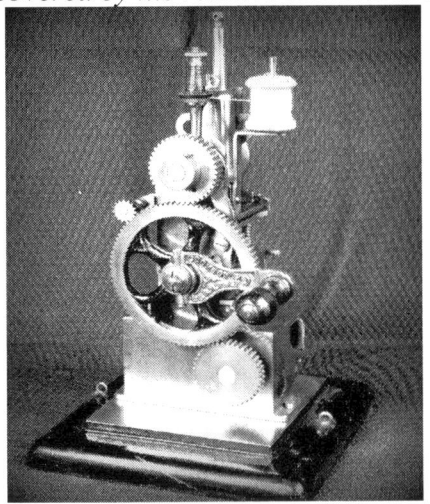

I love this Cookson sewing machine mainly because it does not look anything like one! It was made on clock making machines and it shows. It was never a great stitcher but it is a collectors dream and in my Sewalot Collection.

Like this model toy car? Actually it's a full sized buggy. One of my customers, David Powell, is an upholsterer who specialises in projects like this. He made the interior for the buggy which was a great hit at the show it was in.

Wherever I go I keep a keen eye out for old sewing machines to add to my Sewalot Collection. There is no skill, I just look for old and shiny. There are only three rules to collecting, condition, condition and condition.

Firle Vintage Fair has become a bit of a must see every year. Firle Place, the home of the Gage family, dates back to the time of King Henry VIII. Jane Austen's Emma was filmed there in 2019. The house became Hartfield. It was remodelled in the Georgian period and provided the perfect setting for the film.

The Litlington White Horse at Hindover Hill, near Seaford, is one of the chalk carvings that dot the South Downs. No one is quite sure who first made it but locals regularly maintain the horse. You can make out the snaking River Cuckmere in the valley below.

Archaeologists are often on the Downs digging up bits & bobs. They can find anything from just about any age of man up there. At Boxgrove, further along the Downs towards Chichester, they found early human fossils dating back over 500,000 years. Here are my neighbours Sandra and Freddie at Wilmington just along from Eastbourne. Behind them is the Wilmington Giant, at about 230ft it is the largest chalk carving in Europe.

I Should Be So Lucky!

What does my toothbrush dropping down the loo have to do with finding one of the rarest and most beautiful sewing machines on the planet? Well, let me tell you.

That's how my day had started, with my toothbrush rather majestically bouncing from one side of the loo seat to the other before diving like an Olympic champion straight into the loo bowl. I looked down at it and sighed. Another Monday had begun! The morning didn't get much better, the traffic on the roads was furious; horns blasting, tyres squealing and tempers fraying as huge queues of humans reluctantly rushed to start their working week.

My first customer, an old farmer, had a tricky Brother industrial buttonhole machine which he gleefully informed me 'Once worked'! "I've been told if anyone can get her working it's you, so there she is. Call if you need anything, I'll be down the bottom field." I was left staring at one of the most complex industrials ever made and wondering why farmers always had a bottom field. Before the rise of the computer (which has made sewing machines far easier to repair), complex movements like buttonholes had to be made by a series of levers and cams all working in perfect harmony to create the perfect stitch. This Brother had the added bonus that once it had made the buttonhole, it also cut the hole in it.

I took my jacket off, rolled up my sleeves and got to work. Two hours later the machine made her first buttonhole. "Well I'd never believed it unless I saw it wiv me own eyes. That old bugger ain't sewed a stitch fer twenty years and you've got her working. You know what they say about you is true! You're a bleedin' genius. I'll fetch yer money and tell the missus." With that the old farmer skipped up his drive as if he had drunk six cans of Red Bull.

I drove down his long farm track wondering if I was passing his bottom field and headed for my next customer, praying it would be a simple repair. No chance. Her husband 'the engineer' had spent the best part of a year tinkering with a Singer 760 Touch'n'Sew (which had promptly been renamed in the trade as the Touch'n'Throw). It was a minefield of timing points and micro engineering that, when perfect, would blow your mind, but after forty years of use would often make you feel like actually putting a gun to your head and blowing your mind out!

I retraced all the husband's efforts (with his running commentary beside me as I worked) and eventually got back to the starting point of his tinkering, discovered what was wrong, and fixed the machine. "I knew it was nothing much," he exclaimed as his wife came into the room. I just smiled.

By now my head was spinning. Concentrating for several hours at my age takes its toll. It was near lunchtime and I was making my way back to Eastbourne along The Ridge in Hastings. I suddenly remembered a new bypass that could skip me around the seaside towns and drop me down the old Herstmonceux Road towards home, but halfway along the bypass I missed the turning and was now pointed towards Bexhill on Sea. There was no way to turn around, so I headed for the seaside town to take the coast road home.

Life is sometimes like that, isn't it! It seems to throw lemons at you and if you don't like lemonade you just put your head down and carry on. Sitting in a queue waiting to pull onto the Bexhill Road a flashback of my Mum sprang to mind. "I decided to call you Alex because Alex is a lucky name. If I had listened to your father you would have been called Napoleon. See, that's how lucky you are already!"

I was smiling to myself when I suddenly remembered that my old café-come-antique shop had changed hands and I had not tested the new coffee machine. Because of a series of mistakes (or fate as it turned out) I was now pointing directly towards Bexhill Old Railway Station, where the antique store was housed. It was once called Eras of Style, an amazing place where I often picked up some spanking old sewing machines. The owner, Andy, was a cross between Lovejoy and Flash Harry (the crafty dealer from the St Trinian's films). He was a regular on television shows and they loved filming at the old railway station because it was usually crammed with artefacts from bygone eras. Andy was always up for a good deal, so it was a sad day when he moved. However, now that fate had taken me down the wrong road, I had decided that today I would introduce myself to the coffee machine and the new owner.

The establishment was now called Sivyers Auction Rooms. Bexhill West Railway Station is a stunning building. It is built in yellow and red brick with wonderful Bath and Portland Stone ornamentations around the entrance and windows. It was originally designed in a grand style to become a major railway terminus to compete with the bustling seaside resorts of Eastbourne and Hastings. However she never quite made it. She was opened in 1902 with much pomp and ceremony and quietly closed in 1964 as part of the Beeching railway cuts. What was left behind was a beautiful shell with ornate wood carved panels and doors, and even better for me, a coffee shop. Nothing sparks up my failing brain cells quicker than good coffee.

I was sipping my drink when I spotted a sweet Singer 27k sitting on a table. Now that was a keeper. I examined the machine, which was on sale for £85 and decided to find the owner and make an offer. Mark Sivyer was sitting behind a huge Edwardian desk, tapping away on a keyboard. I asked if he was open to offers and he smiled. Of course he was. Any dealer worth his salt loves to bargain. As long as you master the technique of keeping the banter light and friendly it can be fun. Anyway the dealing halted at £55 and we were both happy. I shook Mark's hand. My bad day was turning at last!

That's when my world changed. "I have another old machine if you would like to see it. She's a bit rusty but the handwheel turns. It's in our first auction next Friday."

The next thing I know, Mark is dragging furniture this way and that, and unlocking doors to a huge storage room. We make our way to the back of the room where a large bust of Cleopatra is staring at us AND something truly amazing! Mark picked up a small ornate sewing machine and handed it to me. In the poor light I first thought my eyes were playing tricks. I had heard about this machine. I had read a little about it in Geoff Dickens amazing book on 19th Century British Sewing Machine Companies, BUT I never expected to see a real one. In my hands was a William Campion 'Lady' sewing machine. It was cast into the shape of a mythical fish out of some Greek or Roman fable. I was like a gold prospector who had spotted a huge nugget shining up from the river bed. However in reality the Campion 'Lady' sewing machine was far rarer than any gold not in value but scarcity. There was only a handful of these beauties known to survive and now I was staring at one!

I started to shake and realised I might drop the machine. I quickly put it down. "It's our first auction, so we are testing the water." Mark added. "Martin will be the auctioneer and Neil will handle the paperwork. This is lot 50."

"What reserve have you set?" I croaked.

"Oh fifty quid I think. We're not expecting much on our first auction."

My mind was racing, but I had to appear calm. I quickly pointed to Cleopatra. "She's a real gem. What's the reserve on that?"

"Twenty to thirty I think. Viewing is next Thursday and the auction starts at 11.00am sharp on Friday. Do you fancy a punt then? It should be fun."

I found myself standing outside the station wondering if what had just happened was real. Now, we all know it's always someone else that wins the lottery, catches the whopper fish and backs the horse that comes first at the Grand National. Mumsie might have given me a lucky name but I'd have to help it along if I was going to get this prize. Nine times out of ten I have lost at auctions or paid a stupid price. As I drove back to Eastbourne my mind was engaged at warp speed.

First things first. I phoned to see if I could buy Cleopatra before the auction (not letting on what I was really after). No, that was out of the question as the lists had been printed and the auction room closed. Great, that also meant no one else could get her either. Could I place a bid online? No, they were not online. NO WAY! Not online! Had I stepped back thirty years? It was music to my ears. Could I view the piece before Thursday? No, it was locked away and not opened again until viewing the following week. Perfect. Next problem. They wanted cash or payment on the day. Funds needed sorting and a price needed to be set in my mind. How much would I pay for a near perfect, complete, and extremely rare machine? Next problem, Eastbourne Airborne would be on and up to 750,000 visitors could jam the roads, stopping all traffic in and out as they try to get to the beach for the air show.

Over the following days all the stars started to align. Yana and I decided to go to £1,000 for the machine and the cash was arranged. I would also take another fifty quid in case I buckled! I dragged out my old Vespa and took her for a spin around the block. Unless a hurricane hit us, I would use the bike to get in and out of town. The days dragged and one night I even dreamed of the Jenny Lind and the Lady sewing machines, the two Campion models I adored. Thursday morning I found myself bombing along on my little Italian wasp, heading for the auction rooms and their viewing day.

As I got to the old railway station, the car park was full. Not a good sign for me, and the viewing had not even started! I squeezed my bike between two cars, walked in and stood in the queue to register to bid in the auction. I was handed number 113. I don't like the number 13, never have. So now things had started to turn back the wrong way. A packed viewing room, an unlucky number, and some old sod already touching MY sewing machine! Didn't he know it was mine! Mine all mine! Calm down Alex and play it cool. Wander around a little. Go and have a look at Cleopatra. I'm sure she won't mind. I kept glancing backwards and as soon as my machine was put down I shoved my way through the crowd and stood staring once again at the wonderful delight.

How on earth did they even make the cast iron castings so delicate but strong enough to last 150 years without damage? Who came up with the idea of using the tail of the fish to hold up the needlebar assembly? To an avid sewing machine collector, since a child, this machine was poetry in motion.

Suddenly two old cronies started shoving me with their pencil-sharp elbows. I had to move away. I stood behind the little devils as they examined the machine. "I told you it was sweet, Gladys."
"Bit rusty, Gertie. I mean, how are you going to clean that?"
"Never you mind how. Just keep an eye out while I push it behind the biscuit tin."

The sneaky old goat! A thought rushed through my mind of just grabbing it and running. At 63 I probably wouldn't make the door before a coronary took me down, or one of those old goats with their Zimmer frames. There was nothing for it, I had to back away and leave the machine till the auction the following day. On my way out I overheard Mark saying to Neil that some of the Corgi cars had been stolen already!

I didn't sleep that night and by four in the morning I was pacing. The clock dragged till nine before I cracked and we set off, two hours early! The auction room was packed. So packed that there was standing room only and I found myself jammed into a corner behind a large, smelly bearded man in a dirty T-shirt and braces. Going by the tattoo on his arm he loved his mother though! I tried to look around him but it was impossible. It was almost eleven when I made my move. I slipped on my bright baseball cap, grabbed Yana's hand and pushed through the crowd, walking straight up to the auctioneer, who was in the only clear space of the room. "Morning Martin," I shouted above the din, "Looks like it's going to be a busy one."
"Busy but fun," Martin gestured back, as he climbed up a few steps so that he could be seen by all. Good, I had his

name right and made eye contact. He would now recognise me as I bid, well my baseball cap anyway. I had picked that little tip up off the TV and it always works like a charm. It is the one essential ingredient in successful bidding at an auction, that the auctioneer can clearly see you. We backed off into the crowd until I had a perfect line of sight and waited.

I have had a bit of auction experience but none of it that good. I ended up paying over £600 for a Tabitha sewing machine hardly bigger than a matchbox. It should have been half that. Then I spent a fortune for an Arm & Platform near Birmingham. Mind you, that was a stunner. I was nervous but that was a good thing. It would keep me on my toes. The auction started fast. Lot one, two, and three. This wasn't going to take long. I made a few practice bids to get used to Martin looking my way (I ended up with a plaster statue of Thomas Moore and the biscuit tin that Gladys and Gertie had tried to hide my machine behind (both would be sold again as soon as possible). I missed a lovely Victorian sewing box and Cleopatra went way above my price. A set of superb Dutch tiles sent the room wild and turned out to be what my beard & braces man had wanted.

Even if you have never been to an auction before you will know that auctioneers have a gavel, a wooden hammer with which to smack the table to signify the winning bid. What you may not know is that the second that gavel hits the table, that 'bang', seals the contract between the auctioneer and the bidder. If the auctioneer misses a bidder's signal and strikes the gavel to an opponent, it's too late. There are no second chances. If you don't signal clearly or he misses your nod, you've lost it. Bidding stopped while one woman complained that Martin had missed her signal. "Too late darling, scream and shout, but when the hammer goes down I'm afraid that's it." Suddenly it was Lot 49. My heart was pounding so hard the 113 paddle in my hand was bouncing up and down like a fan. Then lot 50.

"Lot fifty, a nice old sewing machine called The Lady. Who will start me at ten pounds?" Gladys shot her paddle up. Blimey she was fast! No arthritis in that old shoulder. The bidding went up like lightning. I panicked and found myself just holding my paddle up. I wasn't going to let it down for a second. I was also ready to scream if Martin made a move with his hammer. Ten, fifteen, twenty, up, up, up. Each time Martin glanced around the room, then to me, to see if my paddle was still raised. Forty, forty-five, fifty, fifty-five. I was determined to keep that paddle raised through hell and high water. Suddenly Martin called out, "One hundred and thirteen. Fifty five pounds." He bent over to write on his pad. "Now, Lot 51 an original Harrods box, do I see five pounds anywhere?" I looked around with a confused look. I turned to Yana and she whispered "You've just won it. For fifty-five pounds." I couldn't understand it. I had a pocket full of cash and still assumed I would lose. However it was suddenly mine. I wasn't convinced! As soon as Martin handed the auction page to Neil, we followed him out. Gladys gave me the 'pig eye' as I passed. I'm sure I could hear her hissing! I went to Neil's kiosk and asked him what I had won. "Let's see now, paddle one-one-three, a biscuit tin, a plaster bust of Thomas Moore...terrible hesitation..., oh and a sewing machine."
"I'll pay now!" I almost shouted.

As much as I would have liked, I couldn't touch the machine until the auction was over. With hundreds of lots it would be a long day. Neil said to pop in first thing Saturday to pick it up. The next day before nine we were at the door. I had visions of one of the old dears sneaking it under her coat and disappearing but I need not have worried. Mark

brought out the machine. "I thought it would go for about fifty. I'm usually right. Not much demand for old sewing machines. Is there?"
"Well, I can tell you I love it," I replied.
"Would you have gone higher then?"
"Oh, on the right day yes, I would have gone a little higher."

Outside the auction rooms, Yana got a quick snap on her phone and we headed home. She explained that although I had said I would stop at a thousand, she had brought more to carry on the bidding so that we didn't lose it. I smiled. It always surprised me how much she supported my sewing machine collecting.

Fate has a strange way of dealing the cards, hasn't it! What had started as a bad day, wrong turnings and a toothbrush down the loo, had ended with another wonderful sewing machine in my Sewalot Collection. I glanced across to Yana, who was holding the sewing machine on her lap like a puppy. "I'll have to get hold of the funeral directors when we get home, Yana."
"What are you on about?"
"Well, I'll need the coffin adjusted again so that I can clutch this baby. When I go, she's another one that's coming with me!"

The Lady sewing machine by William Campion is one of the most beautiful pieces of Victorian engineering that you will ever see. The machine is in the shape of a mythical fish and the tail holds the needlebar. It is one of the finest machines in my Sewalot Collection.

The most famous sewing machine of the 19th Century besides Singer was the fabulous Willcox & Gibbs. These machines were simple single thread chain stitch machines with wonderful elasticity in their seams. This meant that clothing stitched with one of these fitted the figure better and moved better. Another point of interest was that the inventor Gibbs made the machine in the shape of a letter G for his initial (when viewed from the back). This became the most widely copied chain stitch sewing machine ever made.

Off The Beaten Track

It is a certifiable fact that no place on Earth is as beautiful as England in the springtime-it needs to be! The human soul (or if you like, our batteries) drain over the lengthy winter months. The long cold nights and short bitter days slowly drag all the spark out of us. The wild banshee from the cold north countries howls over the hills and screeches through the bare trees. She tugs your clothes to let the wind in and slips your woolly hats up for the wind to pierce your ears with its icy chill. We all suffer. For months England can be an awful place, broken by just enough sunshine to keep us alive. There's probably a hundred diagnosable illnesses attributed to winter, but no one talks about the remedy. That remedy is a sunny spring day, when the petals of the early crocus and celandine open and bow in homage to the sun.

I was smelling some wallflowers at my gate when I spotted (too late) the moody old goat who lives at the bottom of my hill. She walks past most mornings, never acknowledging my existence, more interested in the cracks in the pavement than me. However, on this glorious spring day she looked up and, lifting a million deep wrinkles into the broadest smile announced, "What a beautiful day, Alex." She didn't wait for my dumbstruck reply as she strode on with the energy of a Swiss alpine walker. How did she even know my name? I thought perhaps I had better not think of her as the old goat who lives at the bottom of the hill anymore, until I find out who she is! She'll probably turn out to be a relative!

I sparked up the Suzuki and hit the traffic on the main road out of Eastbourne. For 25,000 miles the car had not missed a beat and I was slowly gaining respect for her after losing my great old Land Rover.

Everywhere takes longer to get to now, what with thirty years of migration with hardly any improvements to our infrastructure. Old roads that were laid down by the Romans are now carrying huge trucks and a million cars. By the time I passed Uckfield I was yearning for hot coffee. I swung off the Haywards Heath Road, down a slip road to the ancient village of Fletching, built on the outskirts of Ashdown Forest.

Dropping off the main drag the roads instantly quietened. The church, St Andrew & St Mary, on the corner of Fletching High Street, had daffodils bursting out of the graves and sweeping rows of snowdrops dancing in the early breeze. The church originally dates from the 12th Century. It was at the church that Simon de Montfort and his barons held vigil in 1246, before the famous Battle of Lewes that changed England forever, leading our country to become a democracy. I've written about the battle many times in previous books. However, a little interesting fact I learned recently was that several of Simon's fallen barons were supposedly buried in full armour around the church.

As I drove up the middle of the High Street, full of black and white timber framed buildings, it was as quiet as a church mouse with slippers on. In medieval times Fletching was a centre for blacksmiths and metalworkers who specialised in the production of arrowheads, bodkins and chainmail. What is less well known is that the village was also a centre for skilled leather workers. I had the pleasure of working for one of the old Fletching families for many years. So skilled had they been at everything from quivers for arrows to boots and shoes that they ended up with one of the largest houses in the High Street.

North of the village I pulled into Bell Lane, then on to Witches Lane. There were no signs of witches but plenty of spring, which was bursting out all over. Off the beaten track nature ruled once more. I could see the birds on the bare-leafed trees and sheep nibbling on the first shoots of new grass. One of the great things about early spring is the panoramic views before they are stolen by the leaves.

I rolled onward, ever closer to my first call, past our own little Sheffield Forest here in East Sussex. It is small compared to the much larger forests further up country and I doubted that Robin Hood and his Merry Men would visit; though on this day it would have been a good place for them, for suddenly I spotted a group of deer. I slid quietly to a halt to watch them as they moved along the edge of the tree line. A low mist, which only appears on the softest of early spring days, was hanging a few feet above the grass. The deer were moving slowly through it, making swirls as they went. They stopped every few yards to nibble the new growth. It was a timeless scene. They were rare Roe deer, the only truly native deer that live in Ashdown Forest.

We have loads of deer in the forest and all the surrounding areas, Fallow deer, a few Japanese Sika deer and even the odd Asian Muntjac deer, that have somehow come to live here. However, it is the Roe deer that are the real locals. In the summer they wear reddish coats but in winter they switch to heavier coats of grey, pale brown and sometimes even black.

The Great Storm of 1987 had cleared huge swathes of the forest, allowing all sorts of greenery to grow, which the deer thrived on. Consequently, even with culling and poaching, the deer numbers have rocketed. Several hundred get wiped out every year by traffic racing along the forest roads, but this 'extra' cull has done little to slow down the deer numbers. The deer that I was looking at on this beautiful spring morning were a group of young ones. They have different characters to the others and are fiercely territorial, protecting their feeding grounds. The deer would have been direct descendants of the ones that King Henry VIII would have chased out on his morning hunt. Then he would retire for lunch and later a bit of courting with Anne Boleyn at Hever Castle (which is on the far side of Ashdown Forest. With fresh venison on the menu of course).

A few of my local customers who inhabit the ancient forest lands, have to by law cull a certain number of deer, depending on how much land they own or rent. I think it may be two deer per hundred acres. Of course most of the meat ends up in the local butchers and pubs (probably much as it has done for a thousand years). I have collected many a deer horn from my regulars on my visits over the years. I use them for walking stick handles, buttons and other little trinkets.

As I was watching, a cuckoo called, its sound echoing through the empty forest. It was very early this year. It meant summer was moving up from Africa, well ahead of normal. The cuckoo's untimely call meant the seasons would probably move fast this year. A car stormed by at the speed of light, shattering the calm. The startled deer bounded away like rubber balls, disappearing into the forest in seconds. I sighed, put my camera away without taking a shot and made my way to the first call of the morning. As much as I hate the modern traffic, I love the sights and sounds you see off the beaten track. When I am ruler of the World, one of my first declarations is that nothing is allowed to travel along country roads faster than a 1957 Ferguson tractor!

I neared Woolpack Farm and spotted James Carey, my first customer of the day. He was standing by the cattle grid with his breath trailing up into the cold blue. His collar was pulled tight around his neck. "Cold but bright this morning, Alex" he shouted, as he waved me into his yard. It was more of a statement than conversation. I smiled and pulled up next to his old barn where he worked.

James makes and supplies high class work to shops like Carvills in Uckfield. He is always in demand (as all great quality workmen usually are). In the hard cut-throat upholstery trade, with huge competition from cheap imports, James is one of the few survivors. "I didn't even have time to shave this morning, Alex. What with you telling me that you're coming before the lark! And you're not even on time! The church bells rang a good minute ago!" We both laughed. Arriving only a minute late was a spectacular event with all the traffic nowadays.

I got down to work on his Brother B755 industrial sewing machine, surrounded by all the trappings of a busy upholstery workshop. Off-cuts everywhere, a cutting table piled high with chairs, foam and fillings, all at precarious angles. Settees lined up against the wall, waiting patiently to be restored like customers in a supermarket line. Three nail guns, a compressor, rolls of fabric stacked in one corner, tacks, glue, piping and trim, here there and everywhere. A proper busy workshop. I doubted if I could find a thing if asked. I knew James could put his hand on exactly what he wanted, when he wanted.

By 10.00am I had wiggled my way up to Nutley; then along the High Street, forking off to the Crowborough

Road. Up the B2026, skipping along The High Road and Chuck Hatch Road, which skirts Five Hundred Acre Wood (no sign of Winnie or Tigger today). A quick left turn then by New Bridge Mill. It's only when there are no leaves that you can catch a good view of the beautiful New Bridge Mill House and the old mill pond. A falcon was optimistically chasing a blackbird across the mill pond with little hope of catching it. Once the blackbird reached the bare-branched trees it easily outmanoeuvred the falcon. Luckily for the bird that it wasn't a sparrow hawk or it would definitely ended up as breakfast. The sparrow hawks ability to twist through the thickest of woodland at high speed is a sight to behold. Then I rolled along to my next customer, waiting for me at Coleman's Hatch.

The villages and hamlets in my area ending in 'Hatch' were the original entrances to Ashdown Forest, when it was an enclosed 'royal' hunting forest. The 'hatches' were the only way in and they were well protected by the foresters, working for the king or queen of the time. A quick repair to a Janome Memory Craft and ever onward.

By 11.15am I was working in Uckfield on a beautiful old Singer 66k, made in 1928 at the great Kilbowie factory in Scotland. The Singer machines made before the depression era of the 1930's, and the austere post war years of the 1950's, were made to the highest quality possible. Made first, priced later. I doubt if we will ever see quality engineering to that standard again. I mean, if you think about it, how many items made today will still be working perfectly in a century? Not many.

The Singer may have been a grand old dame but she came up like a dream. I showed off to Diane Stobart with my amazing treadling techniques. Now, if you've never seen a fat old man use a treadle while holding a cup of coffee in one hand and guiding the work with the other, just imagine a clown at a circus on a tricycle, juggling, and you'll be close!

Diane had recently turned her creative skills from quilting to lampshades and, as I had a guided tour of her amazing work. I fell in love with two, a silk hedgehog shade and a linen kingfisher. A deal was soon struck and I bartered my work on her sewing machine for the stunning kingfisher lampshade. No time to dilly-dally, I had many miles to go and still no money for fuel. I had one cheque from my customer in Coleman's Hatch. James was paying by one of the modern scourges to the self-employed, a bank transfer, and I'll have you know that lampshades give very poor mileage!

The day had been going fine but as lunchtime loomed I was running almost 30 minutes late. Something I hate but these days with all the traffic, roadworks, cameras and other hold-ups, there was little I could do about it. My energy was low and I still had two more calls before I could turn the Suzuki homeward bound.

I made my way to a new customer who lived in a plush retirement block in Crowborough. There was loads of parking by the flats but the signs made it quite clear that tradesmen needed to park elsewhere. I drove out again and parked, picked up my backpack (which I have just for treks like these) and walked from my car up the steep slope to the front doors. Huffing and puffing like an old pack donkey, I rang the intercom system. "Hello, its Alex here," I announced in my best upbeat voice, "I've come to repair your sewing machine."
"YOU'RE TOO LATE," a nasty, shrill voice replied before going dead. It was if a hand had reached out from the intercom and gone SLAP, SLAP, SLAP. In that split

second a thousand thoughts raced through my mind. How hard it was to get anywhere on this little island with 70 million other people all pushing and shoving. How the cars behind me were getting closer and closer to my bumper. The drivers seem to want to climb into the car with me now and choose my music! And most importantly of all, how some people still had a Victorian attitude, completely unaware of others! They were used to staff and giving orders. I thought how the days of Downton Abbey were long gone and how this stranger could no longer evict me from my cottage to starve on the streets, all because (as hard as I had been working all morning), I was running 30 minutes late.

As all these thoughts raced through my brain, I had not replied to the intercom. My silence was answered by the door buzzer sounding, unlocking the doors. My customer must have changed her mind! There was a big shiny camera on the system so I knew she was looking. "COME IN, WIPE YOUR FEET, SECOND FLOOR. THE LIFT IS NOT FOR TRADESMEN." Shrieked the orders. However my feet didn't need wiping, they had other plans! They had already made up their mind and turned towards the car. I walked downhill, back to where I had parked. My first contact with my new customer would also be my last! She could get someone else to repair her machine and I would move on to my next call, catching up on some precious time. I could hear her high-pitched squawks all the way down to the road. It's rare but weird how complete strangers can sometimes instantly strike a nerve. I had realised years ago that most of the Human Race get along famously but there is a dreaded three percent that will drive you insane! They often make more trouble and noise than the rest of us put together. I just had a close encounter with one and probably a lucky escape!

At my next customer I was warmly greeted by my favourite sound, a kettle boiling. "The kettles just boiled, you're spot-on time, young man." I love it when I'm called young now that I am in my sixties! "How did you do it with all the traffic?"

"Ah, just lucky I guess," I replied with the biggest smile, knowing exactly why I had caught up.

I was shown into a sweet, well-presented dining room straight out of a 1940's film set. Sitting on a polished medium-dark oak table was a lovely old Helvitia Swiss sewing machine. Awhile later my customer came in with a tea tray with two cups and a plate of biscuits.

I was famished and tucked in. All was right with my little world once more. "Oh there's probably not much wrong with the machine," my customer said as she put the tray down. "My sister and I had it serviced a few years ago."
"Great," I replied, "although," I quickly added, "I can see from here that it won't sew. The needle is in the wrong way."
"Oh, it never worked after 'he' serviced it," she added, "that's why you are here."
"So he didn't fix it?"
"Well," she paused, "that might have been our fault! It was a warm afternoon you see. And, err, we may have given him a little too much sherry! I came in and found him snoring over the machine! We had to ring his sister and bundle him into her car. The next day his car was gone from the drive. He must have collected it during the night. We haven't seen him since, even after repeated calls!"

By now I was sipping hot coffee and grinning from ear to ear. "My sister, Tric uses it more than I do," she continued, "Well, when I say more, she has used it a few times. The machine came from our Granny who lived on the first train stop from the Singer Agents in Stowmarket. She paid for it for over 20 years. Every first Monday of the month she would pop onto the Stowmarket Train with her instalment book and a few bob in her pocket, heading straight for the Singer shop. I remember the machine well as a child, but it was Tric who our Granny taught to sew. Actually my sister's name is Madeline, however every time we called on Granny, Madeline would help with the sewing by turning the hand wheel for her. Eventually she became known as 'Granny's electric'. That got shortened to Tric, and that stuck forever!"

Within the hour the machine was purring. I was hoping to meet Tric and watch her turn the hand wheel, like she had done decades before with her Granny. Unfortunately she was away having a blood test at the docs.

Before I knew it I was on the road again, this time with some cash in my pocket. I stopped at the nearest fuel station before making my way homeward. Most of the day I had been on the back roads of Sussex, off the beaten track, but now I headed straight down the main A22. Another busy day was done and dusted. The sun was in the brightest blue sky and starting its downward curve to its bed for the night, behind the South Downs. God I love springtime, almost as much as my customers (well most of them anyway).

As I drove I shook my head and laughed out loud, an old sewing machine engineer full of sherry, falling asleep over the machine. Whatever next! No wonder I've filled a dozen books with crazy tales; you just couldn't make them up.

Diane Stobart is a master of free motion quilting and her workshop is full of the most wonderful fabrics. This kingfisher lampshade was embroidered with linen and silk. It had to come home with me. Her husband, Mike caught the salmon behind!

Things We Remember

I had a quick stop in town to pop a sewing machine hemming foot through a letterbox, then off to my first proper call up country.

I grabbed a paper from the newsagents in Cavendish Place and was about to hit the road when the scent of bacon came wafting enticingly up the road. I tried to ignore it but found that my feet were moving at a pace towards the door of Cavendish Bakery! I had been popping in there for about a 100 years, well at least 30 since I had found out that one of the bakers had moved there from the famous bakers Bondolfi's along Cornfield Terrace. I had even serviced the owner's old 'Jones' a few times.

With a warm bacon & cheese puff keeping an apple turnover company on the passenger seat, I left town along Upperton Road. I passed two old Eastbourne landmarks, firstly the place where the Maternity Hospital once stood, which is now where the new Allingham Lodge stands, on the corner of The Avenue and Upperton Road.

It was named in honour of our dear old Henry Allingham. The hospital closed and was replaced with Caffyns Garage and an assortment of buildings which in turn had bit the dust and been replaced with super plush retirement homes. Henry was the last survivor from the First World War. As he grew older and older, he passed more milestones. He became more and more famous for no other reason (as he often told everyone) than he was the last man standing. Last man alive from the Battle of Jutland. Last man alive from the Western Front. He eventually became the oldest man on Earth, dying at the tender age of 113! A more humble and shy man it would be hard to find. When my daughter Sarah worked for the papers as a photographer, she often photographed the old aircraft mechanic opening or appearing at local events. Henry became quite used to her and, although hard of hearing, he would often have a little chat. One day at an event he asked Sarah who was the man who kept pushing in on the photographs: "Oh that's Gordon Brown, Henry, our next Prime Minister!"

The Maternity Hospital, which once stretched along Upperton Road, was where most of Eastbourne's babies were born. Funnily all other kids were banned from the place, the result being that there was often a small group of children standing on the corner of Hartfield Road next to the old Flower Land nurseries. They would wait patiently with their dads or grandparents, watching the large window of the maternity hospital opposite. Suddenly a mum would appear and, exactly like the clip out of the Lion King, they would proudly hold the new baby aloft to show their family standing over the road. That was as close as they would get until the new mums were thrown out two weeks later! I stood with my two older brothers and my dad on that corner three times to see my younger brothers held up, leaping for joy when they eventually appeared. The two weeks we had to wait before we could actually hold our new playthings seemed to last an eternity. Sometimes I would creep down the road and wait on the corner just to see if Mumsie would appear with one of my fresh baked brothers. Of course she never did.

Secondly, as I buzzed out of town, I went by my old Sunday Church about a quarter of a mile further along, on the corner of Watts Lane. It was where I attended the Scripture Union Sunday School. It was sadly in ruins. A bulldozer was pulling the last of the beautiful stained glass windows out. It is a sign of our times that these superb old buildings, once at the centre of the community, were being demolished at an alarming rate.

My memories of the place were of fun times. The classes were run by local businessmen, like Mr Verrall, who worked in the Old Town school outfitters where everyone bought their school clothes (before the big chain stores). A white haired, immaculately dressed man who spent his time carefully picking the right size garments for his customers. In the shop he had a pleasant smile and a quiet and calm manner. However out of work his real character shone. To keep the youngsters interested he would break up the lessons with fun activities. The best one by far was the wonderful 'whistling game' and it was very, VERY messy!

A group of kids would all grab a McVities Digestive biscuit from the round tin on the table and stand in a row. When the teacher shouted GO, we would all eat the biscuit as quickly as we could, then try to whistle! The winner was the first one who could whistle properly! Simple eh? No, complete carnage would break out.

Can you imagine the mess and the laughter as we all desperately tried to whistle with a mouthful of dry biscuit! Crumbs were exploding out of our mouths as the rest of the class egged us on with clapping and cheering. We were laughing so much I'm amazed none of us choked to death, except for fat Sam that is, who never bothered to try and whistle but always joined in for the free biscuit! I never won the competition but I bet there were still some of my biscuit crumbs in that old church! Every time I think of that place I smile and see the crumbs exploding out of my mouth as I tried to whistle All Things Bright & Beautiful.

One harvest festival a vicar had come in especially for the service. The small altar was piled high with fresh fruit and baskets of apples. There were pots of jam and chutneys, bunting and straw. The vicar had even allowed some corn dollies, an old pagan nod to Mother Earth. People were coming in with large marrows, freshly baked bread and bunches of flowers, all in all it was beautiful. I was just a kid and I looked on at all this wonder. It was better than Christmas! The vicar explained to us the traditions of the Harvest Festival, that it was for those who had a good year, or harvest, to give to those in need, those who had not done so well in our community.

All these solemn words really sunk in. I reached down into my school blazer pocket (my only jacket, used for all special occasions) and pulled out my lunch, a butter and treacle sandwich, my favourite! I brushed it off and walked to the front, placing it with great importance on top of a box full of bottled fruits. I walked back with pride only to be followed by the vicar. He handed me back my sandwich and patted me on the head without saying a word. I had supposed, in my small brain, no one liked butter and treacle sandwiches! Anyway I stuffed it back in my pocket with a delighted smile. Perfect for lunch in Gildredge Park later.

All my teachers are long gone. Now they have taken the church as well, it is destined for a new community centre, which is great. In reality wasn't that exactly what it was! Nothing seems to stay the same anymore does it? Still they can nick my church but they can't nick my memories.

I stopped at the traffic lights at Eldon Road. I always think that it's funny the things that we remember. Looking back on my long career as a sewing machine engineer there is one incident that is still as clear as a bell. Many years ago, as I started plying my trade, my main worry was how to make ends meet.

One day I bumped into an old aerial fitter. My customer (called Marigold of all wonderful names) had just made me a cup of tea and I stopped to chat to Jim the fitter, who was also having a break. He was sitting on a wooden garden bench munching a cheese and pickle sandwich. His toolbox was next to him with his ladder leaning against the side wall. An assortment of electrical tools were sprouting like carrot tops from of his shirt pockets.

I was desperate to find self-employed people. As we chatted I asked him how long he had been doing the job. I was really after a few tips of the trade, how to deal with customers, holidays, pensions, that sort of thing. It was all new to me and to be honest, scary. I had no idea what path lay ahead. With a young family it was all such a risk to work for myself. I had questioned the decision a million times. He seemed so full of confidence, so self-assured, so peaceful in his own skin. I just had to know why.

It turned out that, although he was top of his class, he left school at 15 and went straight into the trade as a fitter. It was the time that televisions were just becoming available to the normal family so he always found work. As his trade grew so did his reputation. He fitted aerials to big houses and small, to bungalows and flats, any kind of home. If you wanted a television and you needed an aerial on the roof, Jim became the man to ring.

He was semi-retired when I met him but still carried out a few calls each week to pay the bills. He had been there and done it. Survived a whole life as a one man band. I asked him if he ever had any doubts about his life, the money he could have earned, the career he may have had. He laughed and said something so deep and meaningful that it has stuck with me forever.

He looked at me over his sandwich and said, "Son, it makes no difference how much you possess, or how rich you are, the view never gets any better than from the roof of a house!"

It took me a few years to understand what he meant but he turned out to be 100% right. I may not have piles of gold and vacation properties but I've had a life crammed packed full of wonderful memories and even more wonderful (and often crazy) customers.

As the lights popped to green, I selected first gear and pulled away, following the rush hour traffic out of town. Soon I would be at my customer's and there would be no more time to day dream. Would she be an angel or demon? It was anyone's guess. For all I knew there could be a dragon waiting for me with a tongue as sharp as a Japanese sushi knife! Still, decades of dealing with every type of human being had taught me a trick or two!

I smiled to myself, dropped the Suzuki into second, did a perfect 30mph over the brow of Willingdon Hill, waved to the speed camera, and rolled on. I was probably taking the same path out of town that the Romans had tramped a couple of thousand years before me as they headed up country from their mosaic encrusted properties, which had stood near where Eastbourne Pier is today. Anderida may be long gone but I bet the same assortment of characters still exist. Little did I know I was about to bump into a beauty who was going to transport me straight back to the Swinging Sixties!

This is the Upperton Road Reform Church and hall before and during demolition. The land is earmarked for a community centre which is funny really as churches were always at the heart of any community.

Scooter Girl

"Oh Alex, you can't imagine how amazing London was in the 1960's," Denise said as she handed me a cup of coffee. "Thinking back on it now that I'm over 70, it was probably the most exciting time of my life. London was humming. The Beatles were wandering around Abbey Road and Tom Jones was singing The Green Green Grass of Home at his studios. Carnaby Street was a throng of super-excited teenagers pushing and shoving into the fashion shops. Tin Pan Alley was the place to buy an electric guitar and possibly bump into one of the Rolling Stones. I was just a young girl with a love of sewing. I look back on it now as a magical time. Strange, but it all started when my teacher drew a pencil line on a piece of card back at Robertsbridge School."

I love how my stories just turn up, like a magician pulling a rabbit out of a hat. I never know when and where they are coming from. I just set off for work and see what the day brings. I was in a pretty home near Haywards Heath in West Sussex, working on a well-used Juki HZL sewing machine. Denise had started sewing that first day back at her school and never stopped. Here is a golden snippet of her life. I love the part where she loses her false eyelashes bombing along on her scooter.

"Our very first sewing lesson started when we were told to try and follow a pencil line drawn on a piece of card with our sewing machines," Denise continued. "Well it turned out I could not only follow it, but as soon as the teacher threaded the sewing machine, I was away. Sixty odd years later I'm still sewing. I knew before I was eleven that all I wanted to do was sew. I left school the first chance I had and headed on the train for London or 'The Smoke' as we called it back then."

"London was electric, it had a buzz. It's still there, but the city is for the young really, that energy is only with you when you are young. Anyway, I had to shop around a bit but eventually got a job at Frank Usher's as a pattern cutter. Each day I would walk to our little station and commute from my village of Robertsbridge to the greatest capital on Earth. I think I would have worked there for free but I never let on."

"At Usher's they made the latest fashions at a price that would not break the bank. They were on a boom. Wasn't everything in the 1960's! After a customer's measurements had been taken and worked out on pattern paper, it was placed over the fabric. Then I would carefully cut it out. My boss would lean over my shoulder, not in a creepy way, he was lovely, and he would whisper, 'Save me an eighth of an inch on each seam and I'll be rich by Christmas.' It made sense, nothing wasted material more than a badly cut pattern. And with those wasted offcuts went his profit."

"At the London fashion house I learnt my trade. After a year I had earned enough for a deposit on a scooter and that's when the fun really started. They used to call scooters 'hairdryers' because of the buzz they made as they scooted along. At weekends a group of us would arrange to meet up at a pub. We would go out for long rides, down to Hastings or Brighton, or wherever we felt like. I made lovely bell-bottom jeans, stuck on my fake eyelashes and we would hit the open road. My Lambretta had gold panels and went like the wind. No helmets in those days. Only the real hard bikers wore helmets, mainly to prove they were on fast and dangerous machines! Then, the first thing they would do when they removed their helmets was spend forever teasing their 'helmet hair' back up with combs. With my hair blowing in the wind, and often with my leggy sister on the back, we would ride the lanes down to Hastings. Sometimes my false eyelashes would disappear as we went! First job when we stopped was to look into one of the mirrors on the scooter, patch up the white eyeliner and stick new lashes on."

"Now, the sixties were the height of the Mods & Rockers but we kept clear of trouble, and the bad boys in leather. We were much more into dancing than fighting. The real hard nuts would head for Brighton and a fight. The police would be waiting. If it looked like trouble they would call in the fire brigade and 'paddy wagons'. If it all kicked off the firemen would hose down the troublemakers. Then the 'paddy wagons' would cart them away to the cells for the night."

"In reality, many of the Mods & Rockers had spent all their hard earned wages on their clothes and bikes. The last thing they wanted was to get them damaged. We followed the fashion, looked cool, and acted as if we were models on assignment. Sweet Mary, those were wonderful days."

"Of course there was another bonus. Those old paper patterns that we used to mark out the fabric at Frank Usher's were unique to each customer and would normally be thrown away. Well, when I say thrown away, what I mean is folded up and slipped into our handbags to be taken home! The best ones anyway. I would then make copies of all the latest fashions. They would be worn by friends and family around Robertsbridge. We were probably the fashion centre of rural Sussex! It must have made a few eyes pop when people passed through the village, farmer, farmer, farmer, LONDON MODEL!"

"When my parents moved to Haywards Heath I managed to get a job at the world famous fashion label, Jaeger. They had one of their factories in Burgess Hill, just down the road a little. Getting to work was suddenly a breeze. With my cutting experience I went straight to work in the pattern department. At lunchtime I would chat to the sewing girls and pick up their techniques on how to put a zip in quickly, or how to hem a seam without it puckering. You have to remember back in 1970, a Jaeger skirt would cost over four weeks' wages! A staggering amount. But people would save to buy that one special garment. The best news was, twice a year, Jaeger had a factory sale AND the sewing girls had first pick! We would grab some wonderful bargains. I would feel like the queen of the ball on a night out."

"One dance night at a local hall the music was rubbish. There was some awful sounds coming from the latest 'garage grunge', which I think morphed into Punk Rock. I mentioned it to my sister and a lad near me overheard. Well, I was shouting at the top of my voice! He asked what music I liked and I told him I had much better stuff at home. The next thing I knew I was sitting in a 'tuned up' Ford Anglia with no fabric or headlining, no carpet either, but an engine that howled like a monster. It turned out Mike was a racer and the car had been stripped for the circuit. We roared home, then back to the hall with some of my records. When Mike took me back that night my mum told me that if he ever picked me up again, to park a mile away from the house and walk or else! Well, we have been married for over 50 years now. On our wedding day I made my dress and many of the others as well."

"Strange how life is really, when I think of it Alex. It all changed that day when my teacher drew a little pencil line down a piece of card way back in 1960. Now I have so many happy memories. In quiet moments I sometimes find myself smiling, and surprisingly, nearly all of the best ones are because of sewing."

My Patterdale-Border Terrier cross, Cilla, often stands guard watching me work. Everything is so interesting to a young dog. She is by an 1870 Singer sewing machine that was brought back to life for a customer. I used to stack these machines up and take these down the tip most Saturdays when I was young. They are now shooting up in value. I feel like the kid who threw away his Matchbox cars only to find out they are now worth a fortune!

William Terriss was the Brad Pitt of the day, a foremost star of the stage and the biggest box office draw in Victorian London.

William Terriss Murder!

When I was researching my book on Eastbourne called Building A Dukes Dream, I came across an amazing and tragic story that ended up saving countless lives. The story is about one of the most famous actors of the Victorian era, William Terriss.

Out of all the properties in Eastbourne, none has a more fascinating tale attached than that of the Lifeboat Museum along our seafront promenade. Although today it is a museum and shop it was originally intended as a lifeboat station. From 1899, for the first few years of its life, the lifeboat station was home to the James Stevens No 6 Lifeboat.

However, before we explore the strange and gruesome tale of how the building came into being, let me set the scene of a murder that shocked Victorian England, and how Eastbourne ended up with a lifeboat station in the wrong place!

William Terriss was a theatre actor and the superstar of his day. Long before radio and television, film and mass media, the theatres ruled supreme. Theatre stars were the biggest names in the papers besides the heavily censored 'Royals'. In late Victorian England, no name was greater than that of the handsome actor, William Terriss. His life burnt bright but was tragically and brutally cut short.

He was a Scotsman, one William Charles James Lewin. He took the stage name William Terriss when he decided that it would be an actor's life for him. He quickly rose to prominence with stunning performances from King Henry to Romeo in Romeo & Juliet. By his late 40's Terriss was in his prime and the most exalted actor on the London stage. The ever-youthful looking actor played the hero on stage and in real life after surviving being shipwrecked at sea. In 1885, as a keen sailor himself (serving on Merchant Navy tea clippers) he rescued a young lad from drowning and was awarded a medal. The sailor-turned-actor even had a daughter born on Stanley in the Falkland Islands (more of Mary shortly). This made the actor's star shine ever brighter and his shows became sell out performances. Being the biggest box office draw of the time, theatre owners and impresarios flocked to him with offers.

In December of 1897 Terriss was appearing at the Royal Adelphi Theatre in the Strand, London. A play called Secret Service was going down a storm. As usual the theatre was packed before the start of the evening's performance however, lurking in the shadows at the back of the theatre, was one very jealous and dangerous young man, Dicky Prince. Richard Archer Prince was the polar opposite to Terriss. He was a failed actor who felt cheated. He constantly badgered Terriss for bit parts and Terriss felt sorry for him. He helped Prince with small parts and supported him, but it was never enough. Prince grew darker and darker, making Terriss the sole object of hatred for his own failings.

On the fateful night of 16 December 1897, Prince was stalking the shadows, waiting for Terriss on the back steps of the Adelphi Theatre. As Terriss arrived to prepare for his show, Prince stepped out of the darkness and plunged a knife into his back. As the shocked Terriss turned, he struck again, plunging it into his side. Then as Terriss was facing him he struck the fateful final blow, straight into his heart. For a second Terriss recognised the young man that he had done so much to help and grabbed his coat collars, staring him straight in the face. Prince pulled free from Terriss and tried to run but the scuffle was seen. Passers-by grabbed Prince, ripping off his heavy coat, pinning him to the ground.

Terriss lay dying in the alley lit by gas lamps. His leading lady, Jessie Millward, pushed through the crowd and let out a terrible gasp as she saw him. She adored her leading man and clutched the dying actor to her breast. He was bleeding profusely. Covered in his blood she called to the crowd for silence so that she could hear Terriss, who was trying to speak. As he gasped for breath legend tells that he whispered to her that he would return. He then slumped in her arms with the final words, "Oh God." The greatest actor of the age had been murdered.

At 7.22pm, while theatre goers waited patiently at the front of the theatre for the show to start, Terriss lay dead at the back. One of the stage crew had to go on stage and announce to the shocked audience what had just happened. Several women collapsed. The theatre was cleared and the police arrived to take Prince away. It was a tragic scene that had jumped from the stage straight into real life.

Late editions of the London papers carried the news to a shocked capital. Terriss was so well known it was as if a friend had died. His funeral at Brompton Cemetery was the largest ever seen, with over 10,000 people trying to cram in. His coffin nearly fell as it was buffeted by eager mourners. The Daily Telegraph, who had often covered his plays, started a Memorial Fund in his name. Even as Prince came to trial, more money poured in. Strangest of all was that Terriss's understudy, Frederick Lane, had a premonition of Terriss' death the day before he was murdered. It is said that at exactly the same time he was stabbed, Lane's dog became uncontrollable, scaring the entire household with his howling!

Prince's trial was a farce. Destined for the gallows for a cold blooded, premeditated murder, his defence cleverly twisted the case into one of insanity. For the first time in his life, Prince acted out his part impeccably, twitching and stuttering like a lunatic. At the back of the court, quietly watching proceedings, was Terriss's 26 year old daughter Ellaline.

Prince was found to be insane and sentenced to life in Broadmoor Criminal Lunatic Asylum, where he died in 1936. It caused an outrage at the time, with actors and writers filling the pages of the daily periodicals with their disgust. However all this publicity added to the coffers of the ever growing Memorial Fund. Many say that Terriss's last words were prophetic; his ghost is said to haunt the Covent Garden theatre area to this day.

The Daily Telegraph decided that the money raised would be perfect for a lifeboat station for the Royal Life Boat Institution. Eastbourne was chosen as the seaside town had been a favourite haunt of Terriss, when he had time to spare. At a cost of £1,314 work was completed in 1898. On 16 July 1898 the William Terriss Memorial Lifeboat House was opened in Eastbourne by Her Grace the Duchess of Devonshire. If ever you are down that way the large plaque on the side of the museum makes for interesting reading.

Unfortunately Terriss's lifeboat station was not in the right spot. In stormy weather the largest waves hit the shore directly opposite the station, making it almost impossible to launch a boat. This proved so troublesome that the lifeboat was moved along the shoreline to Marine Parade where they had a shallow shingle beach.

Rather than waste the superb building, the RLNI used the boathouse to house the redundant James Stevens lifeboat as a tourist attraction. This proved so popular that the RLNI decided to open a museum. On 22 March 1937 the William Terriss Boat House became the first ever RNLI museum, and it was opened with much pomp and ceremony by Sir Godfrey Baring Bt (Chairman of the RLNI). Attending was Ellaline Lewin Terriss who had become Lady Ellaline Hicks. The distinct clock above the station was added in commemoration of the coronation of King George VI the same year.

William's daughter had gone on to have a successful career on the stage herself. She later made the transition to silent movies, then 'talkies'. Ellaline did her last film in 1939 called The Four Just Men. As World War Two raged, she joined The Entertainments National Service Association (ENSA), which entertained British troops. In 1940 she did a final tour of the Middle East, returned and retired.

In 1962, the TV personality, Eamonn Andrews surprised her as she painted quietly in her back garden and she starred in his program, This Is Your Life. Ellaline, who had witnessed such tragedy in her life, with her father being murdered, her mother dying shortly after, and outliving her husband, went on to live to the ripe old age of 100. She died at the Holy Family Nursing Home in London on 16 June 1971. And so ends a fascinating tale.

Interestingly, the Lifeboat Museum is one of the only properties along the entire seafront that is allowed to sell merchandise. In line with the original 7th Duke's wishes, no shops of any kind were built. The Lifeboat Museum is allowed a little leeway because of its charity status.

The RNLI Eastbourne Museum and shop was built with funds raised after the murder of William Terriss. It is one of the only buildings along Eastbourne Promenade that is allowed to sell goods as per the 7th Duke of Devonshire's wishes.

Sussex still has many windmills. This is Stone Cross Windmill built in 1876 by Thomas Hunnisett. It was run by Dallaway & Son who were millers and corn merchants. One of my customers lives in the shadow of the mill and has the most wonderful views over Eastbourne.

The Maharajah of Cooch Behar was supposed to have a wife in each of the minaret domed properties along Bexhill seafront. Every doorknocker was decorated with a different design so that he knew which wife he was calling on! It is one of those wonderful local legends unfortunately based more on beer and pub gossip than fact. The Maharajah did stay in Bexhill but there was no harem.

I am always astounded that from this little cocoon made by the mulberry moth wonderful silks are produced. These stunning rolls are from Liberty's in London. They may have the best selection of silk fabric in the world. This is just a tiny selection that went from floor to ceiling.

Brighton Pavilion was built as a seaside bolthole for the Prince of Wales who later became King George 1V. It is a stunning mock Indian and Chinese fairytale building. During the Great Storm of 1987 the main dome collapsed but it was soon restored. Below are the typical seaside bathing huts, these ones are on Seaford Beach. They always make me smile, each one is painted in different bright colours so even on the gloomiest of days they can brighten you up.

These are my beautiful grandchildren, Evelyn and Alena. They light up my life when I see them and are just a joy. As you can see Evelyn doesn't eat as much food as she throws! That's a bowl on her head. Shortly after this photo the pancake somehow ended up stuck to the wall behind!

I wrote a children's tale about a magical sewing machine and it went down a storm. I was amazed when it became a No1 New Release on Amazon. Wonderful stories came in from around the world about how much children, and their parents, loved it. Luckily our postman Dan Stirrups would bring his van up after his rounds and load up the boxes of orders. Amazon now deliver them worldwide direct.

Equinox

I adore autumn with its big harvest moons and the warm winds with a hint of coolness to announce winter is on the way. The farmers working furiously to bring in their bounty. A million things proclaiming my favourite season, from the kaleidoscope of colour to the migrating geese flying over my house each evening, honking at the world. Best of all is when I am driving through the forest and the trees scatter leaves in front of my path as if they are thrilled to see me. This year it happened fast! The dark autumn mornings started with a bang and suddenly it felt as if I was setting off to work in the middle of the night.

It was October and the start of another busy week. Today was a special day and I had been looking forward to it for weeks. I had a booking to a customer smack in the middle of the South Downs National Park, two miles away from the nearest tarmac road. Plus I was visiting Elsie, who was more like an old friend than a customer. She had sold her farm and become a millionaire and I wanted to hear all about it!

As I opened my front door, the first streaks of light were breaking up the blackness. The smell of wood smoke hung heavy in the still morning air. A plague back from the 1950's had risen its stinky head again; the dreaded wood burner. It seems to be fashionable for houses to have puffing chimneys again, whatever the cost to the environment and human life. Chimney sweepers, who had all but disappeared, had sprung back to life to service this resurrected phoenix.

Mother Nature had been smack on time this year. There was a sharp start to summer and another to finish it off. It sounds weird but I actually saw the season change! I had been working hard and pulled over at the Z-Bends at Beachy Head for a well needed rest. I can tell you for a fact, sipping coffee at any car park on the South Downs is the best break ever. The sweeping views across miles of open land and sea fills up the soul, and it was there that I saw summer come to an end. Out at sea, Autumn was coming across the English Channel. Deep dark clouds bursting with lightning were pushing a massive weather front towards Britain.

The date was Monday the 23rd of September 2019 and you could have set your watch by the change. The weather had turned exactly as the day balanced, the Autumn Equinox. These were no cotton wool clouds coming my way, blown on sweet summer thermals, these were apocalyptical clouds from some distant past. Loki and Thor were in a rage over the sea. The blue carpet of sparkling diamonds was being engulfed by a black fury. The long hot summer was going to change with a bang. Those beautiful warm winds that embraced me like an old friend were going to be replaced by a tempest.

Gigantic storms, which had started in the Caribbean, had grown in ferocity along the Gulf of Mexico before battering America. Then they had turned and rumbled across the ocean. They stopped in the Atlantic and then started to unfurl like a cinnamon bun, the tail of the storm heading all the way to my little corner of the world, bringing with it the first heavy rain of the season to break our drought. I rushed home to tell Yana to grab the washing from the line. She looked bemused but moments later the wind started. At first the trees shook a little, but within moments the wind was shrieking like a banshee as it was sliced by the tree branches. Suddenly they were rocking all over the place. I heard my neighbour's fence come down and saw a trampoline fly along Huggetts Lane, closely followed by a wheelie bin trying to catch it up! This was serious stuff. Then down came the rain. The heavy hard rain smacked the plants and walloped my big fig tree leaves like an interrogation.

At first, the water just skated off the rock hard ground. The effect was localised flash flooding. Then, as the ground softened, it started soaking up the rain. The empty reservoirs filled (my water butts too). I had been using bath water to water my roses, with the side effect that they all smelt of whatever bubble bath we had been using! However, the rain just came down, day after day. Then the serious flooding started. In three days, more rain fell to earth than had fallen in the previous three months. Part of Lewes Castle that had stood for around a thousand years collapsed! After a few weeks I'm sure I saw Noah asking directions from a parking attendant in town! Eventually the flooding slowed and, as always with us sturdy humans, we cleaned up, cleared up, and got back to normal. Leaving just the councils to make up excuses and insurance men to squabble over their pay-outs!

As I went to open my gate something shot by my face. I turned to see an amazing sight. At first, in the soft early light, I thought I was seeing a flower fairy (shows how my mind works!). It was actually a rare hummingbird moth. It had come to gather nectar from my flowers. It may have been blown off course by the winds but it was a welcome visitor. I watched the multi-coloured little marvel flit from bud to bud sucking up the nectar. The sight lifted my heart. I had heard about them but had never seen one. I got so close to it that, at one point, it shot up and looked straight at me. It flew around my head and, obviously seeing me as no threat, it went back to feeding. What a treat!

However early I leave now, I get stuck in traffic. It is a modern scourge that can only get worse. In the late 1990's deputy Prime Minister John Prescott, had concentrated on public transport infrastructure improvements, but he had not taken into account mass immigration. In four years over seven million extra cars went onto the roads. The influx of young blood had saved our failing economy and boosted the country in untold ways. A baby boom followed, and then the babies all grew up! I had bumped into a driving instructor that told me by 2018 over a million youngsters a year were now taking their driving tests! The old cart tracks of East Sussex had little chance. Gridlock was the word that came over the radio day after day. There was no way around it, I just had to leave earlier each day and do less calls. Amazingly, a trip that once would take 15 minutes could now take an hour. However there was a light at the end of the tunnel!

In August, Franky Zapata, a clever Frenchman, had invented a hover board-come jet-pack. Amazingly, to demonstrate his invention, he took off in France and crossed the English Channel. He looked like something out of a Bond movie. I was glued to the TV watching him land and immediately thought I'll have to put my order in for one of those beauties! My problems would be over. All I needed was a patch of lawn to land on or a flat roof. I doubted that Amazon would be stocking them any time soon but the future was looking brighter, and I could put my first idea of a horse and cart on hold!

For now I still needed to roll along with everyone else, so I sparked up the Suzuki and hit the road. My new car had performed perfectly for three years in a row; we had travelled thousands of miles along old farm roads and the back lanes of Sussex without missing a beat. I had loved my old Land Rover, but I was bonding with my new girl, spending more time in the car than at home some days! By 2020 I would have paid my last payment on her and she would be all mine. I knew all her characteristics and sounds, how she would stop and how quickly she could pull into traffic. What she could do in the rain, and along a muddy track. Most importantly the grip! I had already worn sets of tyres out, each time replacing them with deeper treaded ones that could grip the sort of roads I travel. My life depended on my car and I now trusted her completely.

I followed the traffic to Polegate, dropped off a bulb and needles then hit the road to Seaford. I puddle hopped my way out of town, deciding to take the back roads along to Jevington rather than the main A27, and through Wilmington. I passed the Eight Bells at Jevington just as the window cleaner had arrived. The pub is so old and low that much of it is below road level. You actually step down into the pub when you enter!

Flocks of goldfinch were feeding on the sunflower seeds at Butchers Hole Bottom, their yellow wings catching in the dull morning light as they darted in and out of the flowers. I switched onto the A259 Seaford Road at Friston Hill, opposite the old cart track to the smuggling hamlet of Crowlink, then rolled along the edge of Friston Forest to Cuckmere Haven. Normally the snaking river is a sight to behold as the road cuts through the hillside above it. The Cuckmere has superb curves. It is renowned as one of the finest meandering oxbow rivers in the World. However, today with the flooding it was just a huge bowl of water, like an overflowing bath.

The meandering River Cuckmere is one of the finest oxbow rivers in the world and a big tourist attraction. The main road skirts down the hillside and this is the view you see from your car. However, it occasionally floods and becomes a big bowl of water. February of 2020 was the wettest February ever recorded and the Cuckmere completely disappeared. The geese loved it!

Interestingly, there was a group of Chinese tourists standing along the towpath by the river. They were all staring at the 'bowl of water' with very perplexed looks on their faces, although it didn't stop them clicking away on their cameras. We get a huge amount of Chinese visitors to the area just to see our 'curvy Cuckmere' and undulating cliffs. Apparently the serpent or snake occurring naturally is unusual and the Chinese love it, even being one of the signs of their Zodiac. Also, some famous Korean pop stars have filmed their songs with the river and cliffs as their backdrop. Tourists arrive by the coachload to walk along the banks of the river, but this group had been disappointed. A bit like going to see the Northern Lights only to find it's cloudy! On a positive note the migrating geese loved it, splashing around at their leisure. Some days the Cuckmere Valley has looked like an Attenborough wildlife programme.

In Seaford, I cut through the back roads of the housing estate, which were once the playing fields of the impressive Ladycross private school. We would regularly play cricket or rugby on the fields that are now driveways and houses. Coming into the estate was a young woman carrying a child while her partner was pushing the pram. Nothing too unusual except the pram was stuffed with huge pumpkins, probably from Dymocks Farm Shop just up the road and probably for Halloween, only a few weeks away.

My first proper call of the day was the cracker I had been looking forward to. I was calling on Carol to repair her 1910 Singer model 66. She lived smack in the middle of our South Downs National Park, way off the beaten track. I made my way along the little concrete path that led to a gate high up on the hill at Seaford Head next to South Hill Barn. She had given me the special code for the barrier. I passed all the other cars and walkers in the car park and, very importantly of course, opened the barrier. I rumbled down a mile of dirt track leading to officially one of the most beautiful places on Planet Earth.

I was alone with the cattle and sheep, making my way slowly down and down to Cuckmere Haven. In the distance I could just make out the chimney tops of the Coastguard Cottages perched on the cliff edge by the mouth of the river. The view that was opening up to me on that wet and miserable morning was simply magnificent. It has been on countless calendars and postcards, films and posters. It was even on the front of one of my books, Sussex Born & Bred. In the far distance the white cliffs started to appear, their white faces looking out over the grey, murky sea. Their tops capped in lush green grass and curving up and down almost as much as the River Cuckmere snakes. The undulating hilltops are quaintly called the Seven Sisters and they stretch all along the coast, from the Cuckmere Haven to Beachy Head, creating a vista that massages the spirit with positive energy. Artists and photographers come from all over the world to try and capture their majesty as the sheer white cliffs drop hundreds of feet to the water below. They are often mistaken for the White Cliffs of Dover, some 60 miles along the coast. They are FAR superior, of course!

I parked the car just off the track, a few yards from the mouth of the river and climbed out to see the spectacular view. A large sweeping bay lay at the mouth of the river. A low shingle bank curved away from me towards the cliffs. It was high tide and the English Channel was lapping at the base of the cliffs which rolled away, disappearing into the murky mists. In the far distance I could just make out Belle Tout Lighthouse perched above Horseshoe Plantation. Ever since I was a kid I had gone there, prawning or fishing. It was a prime spot for Bass in the Spring as they surged up the river to the muddy banks for their favourite snack, red ragworm. Carol called to me from her cottage. Time to get to work, I thought.

Behind my son-in-law, Dominic is Cuckmere Haven, one of the most awe inspiring sights in my area, perhaps the world. You can see the coastguard's cottages behind. In the distance the fabulous rolling cliffs stretch all the way back to Eastbourne.

Her home for 30 years was one of a row of coastguard cottages. It was placed there to stop the smuggling that was rife along our coasts for centuries. It peaked each time the government of the day raised duties on certain goods, from silk to booze, basically creating supply and demand. Smugglers would land on some deserted beach like Cuckmere at the dead of night, and shift hundreds of barrels of grog in a few hours. Actually one of the most smuggled goods was tea, closely followed by silk. Booze could be brewed at home, so although the history books like to tell you it was gin, whisky, and a squirt of brandy for the parson, in reality most of that could be brewed locally. Tea, silk and cigars were another matter altogether.

Also they were much lighter than liquids and heavily taxed for years.

I'll also quickly tell you this as it's fascinating and rumbling around in my weird brain. It was the women who used to do most of the brewing while the menfolk were hard at work. They became the masters of the craft. It was only when the Roman Catholic Church started persecuting them as witches, bent over their cauldrons that men took over and carried on the timeless craft. Strange but true.

There was one local smuggler who loved to dress in womens clothes! James Petit ran the Eight Bells at Jevington, which I had driven by earlier. He would regularly smuggle tea and silk dressed as a woman! Apparently he would layer up in petticoats of silk and tea and waddle his way back to the pub from the beach. On a dark night a customs officer could easily be forgiven for letting a pretty woman pass by on her way home. I don't believe a word of it, but it's a great local legend all the same. Can you imagine some gruff old smuggler in the dead of night, dressed in layers of new silk, stuffed with tea, clomping by in his hob-nail boots! WHO GOES THERE? Comes the shout from the customs men. "Tis only sweet little me, sir. Just on me way 'ome, ain't I me darlin'. Nighty nite."

The home of the best known smuggler in Alfriston still exists. It's called, wait for it, Ye Old Smugglers. I bet that surprised you! The house was originally Market Cross House, right opposite the old market cross, well what's left of it. Lorries have chipped it worse than a one-eyed apprentice stonemason with the shakes. Stanton Collins lived there and ran the infamous and cold-blooded Collins Gang. Legend tells that the gang were responsible for the demise of several excise men, though nothing was ever directly pinned on Collins. The house, beside the cellars and secret passages, had nearly 50 doors! It still has loads today. If the authorities did come a-knocking it was nearly impossible to catch all the smugglers as they ran for the exits. Once out into the pitch black countryside they were safe. I know from experience it is an easy place to get lost in! I went to the loo in that pub once and spent ages opening doors trying to find my way out! No I wasn't drunk! Collins, whose day job was a butcher, was eventually prosecuted for a minor crime and deported to the convict settlement at Port Arthur, a few miles from Hobart in Van Diemen's Land, or Tasmania as it is known today.

Today, the coastguard cottages up and down the country are no longer to house excise men to spot smugglers, but are mainly residential. At her coastguard cottage, Carol had no electricity, no gas, no oil supply and no phone line. She had wood delivered for heating, though she picked up as much washed up driftwood from the shore as she bought. She had one small wind turbine that supplied just enough electricity to charge her mobile phone and iPad so that she could keep in contact with our modern world. In her house were oil lamps and about a million candles. The place smelt of smoke and fresh flowers, which she had picked from the meadows behind her cottage. It's funny how many of my customers live off the grid in this modern age. You would not think it was possible but they're out there. I should know, I visit most of them!

I rebuilt Carol's treadle, gave her a few tips on how to use her binding attachment and hit the road, slowly driving back up the path, chasing bleating sheep away before locking the gate again. I turned and looked back at the beautiful view from South Hill Barn and sighed, sweet Lord there are some amazing places in my area.

My next call was at Gingers Green. As I arrived the hubby was getting ready for an Extinction Rebellion Rally in Brighton, which coincided with the Labour Conference that was also happening there. They had a wood burner burning away in the house and a big bonfire outside. I thought to myself that they had their hearts in the right place but they hadn't really thought through Global Warming and air pollution! I later found out that the rally had left tons of rubbish behind on Brighton Beach!

My last call of the morning was to my millionaire, Elsie. Typical of Autumn, the weather had gone from drab, wet and miserable to warm and sunny. I drove down the old farm track towards Elsie's farmhouse, like I had done many times before, but this trip would be my last. Funny isn't it how when we know we are losing something we take more time to soak it up. I knew that the next time I drove along here it would be a big road leading to an even bigger housing estate with new occupants from all over the country, even the world, all living on the land that the cows were now grazing on.

As I got out of the car, two pigeons that had been drinking from the water trough outside Elsie's farm, raced away as if I had a shotgun, their wings smacking loudly across the open farmland. Within seconds they had cleared the field and disappeared into the far woodland. I shoved my way carefully through the cattle to the farm door, avoiding the messy back ends!

The house had been untouched for years. After Elsie's husband, Sid, had died, she spent most of her time running the farm with her kids. She made ends meet using an old hand Singer and knew the value of a shilling. I've always thought that poverty was a great preserver. Her house looked like it was out of an episode of All Creatures Great

& Small, set back in the 1950's. I expected James Herriot's smiling face to appear from the back end of one of the cows at any second!

However, it was the end of an era for Elsie, and me too, really. The first rows of yellow surveyors tape were staked out over the open fields. Out of the blue an estate agent had knocked on her door. He politely told her that she was sitting on a gold mine, well something more valuable; prime building land. His company could handle everything from planning permission to the sale of the land. They would do everything and she could even keep her house if she wished to stay there. Elsie, who had scraped a living from the land for all of her life had sold it for millions and was now rich beyond her wildest dreams. She then declared that she didn't want to live in a housing estate and announced to her family that she would be moving at her convenience!

As Elsie noticed me in the doorway her eyes lit up. "Oh Alex, what a joy to see you." She rushed over and gave me a big kiss. "Everything changes except you, Alex. Years go by and I pick up the phone and there you are on the other end. My Sid would have loved to have seen you. Six years now. He's been gone six years already! Pancreatic cancer did what those wicked Bosch couldn't. Still I'll tell you something, Alex. He was so brave, always smiling right until the end. His last words were, "Cancer might be killing me Elsie love, but no one said I couldn't go out with a smile!" I cried so many tears after he died. I knew it was coming but it was still such a shock. I had never really cried much before, then the tears came, day after day, night after night. My bed was suddenly so huge and the loneliest place in the world. I would just roll into a ball and cry myself to sleep. Sometimes I would wake and reach out to see if he was there, and then cry some more. Sid often snored so loud that he would rattle the windows. I always moaned at him for that. He would just shake his head and laugh, telling me to prove it! Now I would give my last days to have his snoring back. Eventually the pain eases a little and you realise you just have to soldier on. I pulled myself together, more for the family really. God he was such a treasure. Oh do come in, Alex. What are you standing there for?" She grabbed me and pulled me into the farmhouse like a sack of spuds!

"Have you lost weight, Alex?"
"Yes, two jumpers and a body warmer," I laughed, "Mind you they will be going back on shortly now that the cold mornings have started again. I see that's the last harvest all cut, Elsie" I said, beckoning through the window to the freshly cut field.
"Yes, we worked all our lives from dawn till dusk to put food on the table and now my children will never have to work another day. Not unless they want to that is. No more five o'clock starts or midnight calving. No more worrying if the wheat will ripen or the lambs will survive a late frost. My children, grandchildren and great grandchildren will have all the things I never had. I'm not so sure that's a good thing but my kids are getting on a bit now so they will be able to enjoy their lives like Sid and I never could. Also the great grandchildren can all go to university without being burdened with lifetime loans. That was such a worry and now it is all irrelevant. You know Alex, we never had a holiday. Not one in over 50 years! Now I've booked three weeks on the largest cruise ship in the world. I think it's called the Sea Breeze Harmony or something like that. It's going to be great fun. I don't even know where the Caribbean is but a taxi is picking me up and I'm going there!"

Elsie toddled off to get refreshments and I got down to work on possibly the only heirloom that one of her family may inherit, a Singer model 15k. Funnily, because of Elsie's advancing years, her kids were mostly in their 60's already. I was smiling to myself about Elsie as I worked on her machine. Some people just make you happy, don't they! I spotted her out of the window picking rosehips from the hedgerow and throwing them into a basket slung over her arm. She must have forgotten all about my tea!

I remembered that her Singer had a great story attached. It was her husband Sid who told me the tale a long time ago. He was a big man with an incredibly deep voice. He had spent the end of the war fighting his way through Europe towards Berlin. He didn't actually say, but I assumed he was in some sort of army intelligence, as he told me that he had instructions to search out any military headquarters and grab the paperwork before the Russians got it. Anyway I am digressing a bit (as usual). Not long after Sid had returned from the Second World War, Elsie fell pregnant.

Interestingly, the cold winter nights of 1946 and the returning servicemen triggered one of the largest baby booms in British history. With the arrival of their first child, Elsie desperately wanted a sewing machine to make baby clothes. Rationing was still biting and fabric was scarce, however old clothes and curtains could be unpicked and made into all sorts of wonderful things for their new baby.

They had heard that Steele's, the sewing machine shop in Brighton, had a Singer for sale. They wasted no time and hopped onto the first train that they could. When they arrived they found out that it was an old 1890's treadle. Mr Steele was out but the shop assistant mentioned that he had just gone to look at another sewing machine to buy. She suggested that if they would like to come back in a few hours he may have some news. Well, all afternoon Sid and Elsie argued about the old treadle. Elsie hated the idea of the old machine, as it would have to go in the small room that they were keeping for the cot. By late afternoon Elsie had decided it would be better to have the old machine rather than none at all.

At the time there was around a two year waiting list for a new Singer sewing machine. By the end of WW2 the Singer Company had back orders for over 3,000,000 sewing machines! They had spent the war making armaments for the forces. Strangely, just like they marked their sewing machine parts, they marked their munitions. If ever you come across a No36 Mills Bomb with SMGC on, it was made by the Singer Manufacturing Company in Scotland! Their .45 pistol, known as the M1911A1, is one of the most collectible handguns ever made. Singer were used to manufacturing premier quality pieces of engineering so, when they made the handguns, the same quality went into them as well. In 2017 one sold for $414,000, one of the highest prices ever paid for a handgun. They only made 500 before they were switched to other products where super-high quality was essential, like bomb sights and gyros. The few M1911's that survive are considered the finest of their type. Now I bet you never knew that!

When Sid and Elsie arrived back at the shop that afternoon, Mr Steele greeted them and took them into his workshop. Sitting in a big bath of paraffin was a Singer model 15k, in pieces. A superb all-round workhorse. Mr Steele promised that it would be theirs. A week later he delivered the machine looking like new. It had been completely restored and repainted with the latest gold Air Force decals. Sid paid two month's wages for it and 73 years later I had turned up to service it once more! Elsie had made everything from her daughter's christening gown to her son's wedding waistcoat. The machine must have sewn a billion stitches. Back in the 1980's I had removed the hand crank and put a motor on it for her, so that she could make some new curtains with ease. It was a common job for me to do back then.

Elsie had just had her 93rd birthday and would be moving to an apartment along Bexhill seafront, where she would be nearer her remaining friends. Out of the few things that she was taking, the old Singer was one. "They all think I'm crazy," she said. "I don't care. I'm the one with the money now. If I want my old Singer, I'll damn well have it! Money can't buy memories eh! As long as I have my Singer I have a little bit of my Sid, too. Now, before you go I have a pot of rosehip jelly for you. I know how you love it."

As I left, the freshly cut fields, warmed by the late morning sunshine, smelt glorious. Swallows and House Martins were feeding noisily over the low cropped stalks. This would be the last harvest that these fields would ever see. I thought to myself how the sound of the 'warbling chirp' of those wonderful little birds was really the sound of Autumn. For the last week or so they had been gathering in large flocks all along the coast, often perching on telephone wires in that classic sight, like pegs on a clothesline. Any day now they would whip along the coast to Dover. Then, as soon as the wind turned, they would shoot the 20 miles or so over the English Channel, and start their epic journey across Europe, off to Africa for the winter.

Sweet mother of mercy, everything is changing so fast around my area. Elsie had plonked a kiss on my cheek again at the door, "Remember the golden rule, Alex. Don't do anything that will keep you awake at night. See you at my luxury apartment in Bexhill. I've kept the hand attachment for the Singer. I might get you to take the motor off and 'retro' my baby. It will look a picture."

As I drove along the dirt track, I almost had a tear in my eye. Still, I need to pay more attention to my crazy old customers who keep telling me to look forward in hope, not back in resentment. On the positive side, I bet Elsie's new place in Bexhill will be amazing. They have converted many of the grand old hotels into plush seafront apartments. I've been in a few and some are mind-boggling luxury, with million pound views. I took some consolation with the image of me on my next visit, sitting on the balcony with tea and biscuits, overlooking the sea. I bet you a month's wages there will be a big picture of Sid on the table, in his army uniform too.

Bondolfi

Once again we are going off the beaten track for this next story. I just have to write it down before it is too late and is lost forever. Actually, as you know, most of my stories are off the beaten track, but great fun. I'm going to take you on a magical journey to a shop where every day seemed like Christmas Day. A shop that, for five decades, from the 1930's to the 1970's, was possibly the best of its kind there has ever been. I've mentioned this shop in previous books, but only fleetingly. Now we are going to discover a long lost masterpiece, well shop. Believe me it's worth the read.

Very few images remain of the fabulous shop Bondolfi, but take my word for it their pastries and displays were famous all the way up to Buckingham Palace in London. It was one of the jewels in Eastbourne's crown for five decades.

In the 1960's Eastbourne of my youth, there were many wonderful shops, all long gone now. Fur shops selling mink coats, which cost as much as a new car; window displays with real fox stoles, elegant models with a dead animal or two wrapped around their necks. Rich old women would buy them with money from their snapping handbags (it's what the kids called their crocodile bags). There were high class haute couture dress shops like Peter Norton's in Carlisle Road, or Driscoll's, who made Queen Elizabeth's, and her sister, Princess Margaret's clothes. Driscoll's once got into a lot of hot water with Buckingham Palace about that (it made a great story for my book 'Tales From The Coast'). There were countless amazing shops before the High Street clones smothered so many town centres. However, out of all the Eastbourne shops, none compared to the amazing Bondolfi, run by the Swiss baker, Adolfi Bondolfi.

I believe the shop first opened way back in the 1930's and within a short time Adolfi and Mary Bondolfi built a fabulous reputation as the best tea rooms in town. During the Second World War, because he was Swiss, he was interned and let out at the end of hostilities. Interestingly, when I was a kid they lived just around the corner from us in 'posh' Prideaux Road; full of doctors, bank managers and solicitors, in large rambling houses. We were in Ashburnham Gardens. By the 1950's the tea rooms were on a roll once again with the best pastries and cream teas in town. They had to be good to compete with the finest hotels along the seafront promenade and the countless other tea rooms, including two Lyons Tea Rooms. It was also the height of the dance era where many hotels offered space, even sprung floors, for afternoon tea dances. In the height of the big band era, Bondolfi put on regular bands and jazz nights at the shop.

Bondolfi's shop was a large double fronted building along Cornfield Terrace. It was no ordinary cake shop, it was possibly the best Swiss patisserie in the country, maybe the world, with a window display to match. As a kid I would drool over the goodies like a street urchin from a Dickens tale. There were rows of Swiss pastries and delicacies from chocolates to cakes, all displayed to delight the eye, and all way too expensive for me. Plates of cream horns with just enough pastry to hold a gallon of fresh whipped cream. Sticky buns, cakes and eclairs would almost burst out of the display windows. However these delicacies were for the Eastbourne Elite and special occasions only. Regulars became known as 'the Bondolfi Set'. They would alternate between the top hotels, like The Grand along the seafront, The Chatsworth and Bondolfi's.

One doughnut, French fancy, cream puff or rum baba in the 1960's would cost roughly two shillings and sixpence.

Actually you had to watch out for the rum babas as they put a double shot of rum in! Not surprisingly, while the adults couldn't get enough of them, it was the only cake that most of the kids didn't like! Now, to understand just how much two-and-six was, for delivering papers, seven days a week on my paper round, I was getting five shillings! So a week's struggle at the crack of dawn, in all weathers, would have bought me just two pastries! Crazy or what!

Even though they had the reputation for the best cakes in town and everyone talked about them incessantly, I only ever tasted one pastry from there, and that came with the most amazing story attached. It was given to me by none other than Doctor Death himself, the infamous Doctor Bodkin Adams. He was associated with hundreds of suspicious deaths, mainly wealthy old dears who subsequently left him nice bequests in their wills. I have his full and scary story in my book, 'Glory Days'. Like I say in it, he arrived in Eastbourne on a bicycle, and by the time of his death he had huge properties, staff, and was being chauffeured around in a Rolls Royce! Still I won't hear a bad word about the man as he was the only reason I ever tasted a Bondolfi doughnut.

I was on one of my 'window shopping' days when he skipped by me, immaculately dressed as always. He stopped at the door and reached down into one of his pockets and pulled out a pound note. One of his strange habits was that he always folded his notes into little squares. As he was unfolding the note, he looked at me for the briefest moment. Dr Adams then bounced into the shop. He was fat but as light on his feet as a ballet dancer. Moments later he reappeared and handed me a bag without a word spoken. He shot away, along the road to his grand town house with a large Bondolfi box under his arm. He only lived about 200 yards from the shop. Inside the bag was the most wonderful jam doughnut ever and still warm! I had jam running down my cheeks and sugar all over my face in seconds. I snuffled it down like a starved monster.

Although Bondolfi might have been out of my price range, staring through the shop window was free, and always a delight. Each morning I would pick up the papers at W H Smiths for my paper round, which was on the main platform in Eastbourne Railway Station. Then I would cycle up to Bondolfi's on my way to Silverdale Road, the start of my delivery round. Then I would return and pick up my second round, which started in St Anne's Road, and deliver it before going to school. Early every morning the staff at Bondolfi would create just the finest window displays that Eastbourne has ever seen. It was their theatre, their art gallery, and they were the artists. The closest I have ever seen to it is the Harrods pastry counter.

Chocolate moulds made in Dresden, Germany, were supplied to Bondolfi from their Swiss chocolate suppliers, Lesme. These were no ordinary sweet moulds. There was a life-size Father Christmas, giant Easter eggs, a giant Easter Bunny, along with loads of little ones; chickens, teddy bears, and chocolate turkeys for Christmas too. Anything from eggs to footballs, all made out of the best chocolate money could buy, and all perfectly displayed depending on what time of year it was. After Christmas and Easter the window displays were often donated to the town hospitals like Princess Alice, my regular, in Carew Road.

They would have the most amazing looking Florentines that you could ever imagine, along with chocolate Austrian Sachertorte, and Stollen. I was told that they made the best Apfelstrudel outside Vienna, which I was pretty sure couldn't be true! Layers of sweet spiced apple rolled in the thinnest, lightest pastry, just to die for. Although I only had the one doughnut from Bondolfi's, my part Austrian mum was a witch with a mixing bowl. She had been trained by pastry experts and could knock up mind-boggling concoctions. It was Mumsie that made the best Apfelstrudel outside Vienna. It used to take her all day and was a thing of beauty when it came out of the oven. It was usually gone in seconds as six hungry boys devoured it although sometimes we reluctantly left a few crumbs for dad.

At Bondolfi's the pastries and cakes were all baked by a team of expert bakers and pastry chefs. Their walnut cakes were stuff of legend, still talked about to this day! People astoundingly also still rave about their wonderful cream sponge, which they called an Othello Cake. It's somehow connected to the Shakespeare play but I have no idea how. It is possibly Danish in origin, but just seeing that cake in the window blew my mind. If you have not tasted one of these then you haven't lived! Put it on your bucket list right this second. The cake was a masterpiece of engineering as well as pastry. Slices of light thin sponge (sometimes plain, sometimes chocolate) brushed with a red jelly jam then built up in layers with thick whipped vanilla cream, crème patisserie and crumbled macaroons. It was topped with shiny chocolate fondant and swirls of more whipped cream. The entire border of cake was then rolled in marzipan. The cake was just a thing of beauty. If you Google 'Othello Cake' that will bring up something similar, then imagine double the layers and double the size. That would be the Bondolfi Othello. These cakes were always so time-consuming and complicated to assemble that they were not on sale every day. They were probably made when the pastry chefs had the time. I would sometimes watch as one of the waitresses would carefully lift a cake out of the window and bring it back moments later, with another slice gone to some lucky customer. God I'm dribbling just writing this down! I think you get the idea. The cakes and displays were just the best.

By the time I was a spotty teenager I was staring through the shop window on a regular basis and Bondolfi's reputation had become nothing short of a wonder. It was always so busy no one noticed me. There was often as many people staring at the displays as were buying stuff. If you imagine the Mad Hatter's Tea Party you would be close to the excited noise and commotion around the place!

Working for Adolfi Bondolfi were several highly experienced chocolatiers, mainly women, who had their own department on the first floor. Bondolfi had a battalion of staff and several pastry chefs, including the master baker, Alex Bransgrove, who made cakes for the rich and famous. He made a spectacular cake in the shape of Herstmonceux Castle for the Formula One racing team, McLaren. He would also create spectacular ocean liners and cruise ships in cake. Even better than that, he made several Royal cakes including one for Lady Elizabeth Angela Marguerite Bowes-Lyon, fondly known as The Queen Mother. It was for her 80th birthday cake in 1980. It obviously did her good as she lived for another 21 years! Alex's daughter, Sylvia Guppy, was a regular customer of mine. When I visited she would often get out the scrap album and show me some of his amazing creations.

At Easter, when hot cross buns were a big seller, you would sometime see the white clad pastry chefs come out early in the morning with buckets of steaming liquid, which they would wash over the pavements. Suddenly the whole area would smell of heaven. They had mixed in spices with warm water to attract customers. How clever was that! By opening time there would be a queue outside the shop. Mind you, most days the place was rammed. Some families would save all year to have a special celebration at Bondolfi's. I always felt a little sorry for the immaculately dressed waitresses who seemed to fly at the speed of light, serving all the tables. In the height of the tourist season when Eastbourne's population would double, it would be like feeding a small army. The logistics of it all were spectacular. For many, a holiday to the town was not complete without a visit to the shop. The great news for the staff was that all the workers in the shop were allowed a pastry of their choice every single day! Like I say, I only felt a little sorry for them, but very jealous.

Besides all the cakes and pastries that lined the windows and the display shelves, they did light meals, soups and a speciality Welsh Rarebit, which was their ever popular version of cheese on toast. Surprisingly they did all the basics too, like beans or sardines on toast and loaves of Hovis bread, which they bought in for the regulars. If the doors were open you could sometimes hear the waitresses shouting to the chefs over the crowd, SIX RAREBITS, TABLE NINE.

Bondolfi also specialised in wedding cakes. Once again they weren't cheap, but they were the best. Many of my customer's memories are just of their fabulous wedding cakes for those special days. They supplied cakes and pastries all over the country and beyond, in beautiful gold wrapped boxes. A few locals still have the boxes as treasured memories of that unique place. I'll tell you something funny, when my school went swimming at Devonshire Baths, which has long gone now, the bus would go past Bondolfi's. Now, if you ever wanted to see a bus nearly tip over, that was the place. To get a glimpse of the cakes as we passed the shop, almost every kid on the bus would leap over to the windows that the shop was on. The road has a nasty camber on it anyway and the whole bus would lean over as we went by. Sometimes the driver and conductor would start screaming at us.

If ever I mention Bondolfi to a local over a certain age, they will suddenly start raving on about the amazing eclairs, or their special tiramisu with double chocolate and Italian espresso coffee, or the huge chocolate rabbits. All in all it was stunning, and all my customers agree that the cakes tasted even better than they looked. And they looked spectacular!

When Bondolfi finally retired in the late 1970's the shop became Zetlands and today it is a bed centre called Mr Beds. Adolfi Bondolfi lived well into his nineties. Obviously all that cream, sugar and butter pastry wasn't so bad for him! It was the end of an era when he retired, and possibly the end of the best cake shop in the entire world.

I often stare in the window of the bed shop when I walk by. I swear if I close my eyes just a little, a magical display of Swiss pastries appear and a short round doctor, in a Savile Row suit and pork pie hat, brings me out a brown paper bag with a doughnut. Wonderful, wonderful memories of old Eastbourne.

Winter Work
Dec 2019

"And exactly what do we receive in return for the extortionate fee you are asking?"

My God I could feel my guts tightening. It was almost Christmas Eve 2019 and I was clearing up my last calls of the year. Emergencies, one after another were being sorted. People who were desperate and needed to finish off sewing for presents or business. These last calls are usually pleasant and welcoming but I had the unfortunate luck to be standing opposite Ebenezer Scrooge in full tilt. "Your wife explained to me that she was donating the machine to a girl for Christmas and wanted it perfect, serviced and safety tested." I explained through gritted teeth. He grumbled, I bit my tongue. I was in his home and manners can often win through.

Some days I feel like I have the best job in the world, other days I think twice! The day had started great, first call to Sarah at the Horam Fabric Shop. Her Juki F300 had broken sewing curtain heading tape into some massive velvet curtains for Horam Manor. Deepest winter is one of my favourite times. The year that has been slowly getting shorter and shorter suddenly turns. From now on, each day a hint of Spring is thrown my way, via birdsong or bulbs sticking their heads up to have a peek and see if the coast is clear. Short days meant that I had left for work while it was still dark and would arrive home after dark. But then gloriously, I would be finished until the New Year.

Each time I get my tools out I have to wait until my glasses clear. They cool down in the car and then steam up at my customers, who often have the heating on as if they live in deepest Siberia, not East Sussex. After Sarah it was off to Buxted Upholstery to sort Paul's Brother B755 Industrial, then up Five Chimneys Lane and the tiny back roads to Crowborough. I passed Coopers Farm and quickly hit the brakes. Mike was just putting out some fresh pork sausages, which I knew from experience were dribblingly scrumptious. I just had to have a pack or two for the freezer. Then up, up, up, along Hadlow Down Road through a tunnel of bare trees coming up in Jarvis Brook, which sits just below Crowborough. Crowborough is one of the highest spots in Sussex but the heavily forested and wooded area steals all the amazing views that it may have had. I remember calling at one customer who had one of the most stunning views I had ever seen, all the way back down to the coast from where I had started my day.

Sometimes you get a clue to a customer before you arrive. Mr Scrooge was no different. His garden path was made up of broken pottery, including a loo bowl! Wow, if ever there was a sign of what was to follow, that was it. The doorbell looked as if it was holding the door together. It didn't work, so I banged loudly on the door and waited. A scruffy man in a cardigan full of holes opened the door. Inside was a mess of waste bags and stacks of rubbish. He looked as if he was a one man recycling team. Then I had the dreadful thought that he had just never parted with anything. Not even a plastic margarine tub! "Wife's out. Here's the machine. Now exactly what do we receive in return for the extortionate fee you are asking?" I went through my sales pitch, wishing that I had turned back at the toilet seat. I wondered if he handed out lumps of coal as Christmas presents! "She's paying out of her carer's allowance. I've got….." My ears faded out his list of ailments as he went into overdrive. I knew just by looking at the way he was moving, he didn't have half of what he was claiming.

It's a point that my doctor made many years ago, which he in turn had been taught to him by his father, who was also a doctor. Look at the way someone moves. It will tell you more about them than they will tell you with their lips! He had perfected calling his patients into his room and watching them come along the corridor while he held the door for them. They thought he was being polite but in fact he was getting the lowdown on them before they had said a word. I can tell you now, no one with a locked shoulder could lift a Bernina Record onto the table the way that old sod did! Luckily, a sweet pearl-haired dear opened the door and saved me. She quickly ushered the old fart away and almost slammed the door behind him. "Second marriage. Who knew what he would become. Still it's all too late now. It's like living with ten men! Nine asleep and one dead! If I didn't get a carer's allowance I think I would have buried him underneath that loo seat he cemented into our path. Can you imagine anyone doing that! Don't answer, I know we are both thinking the same thing! Now Alex, down to business. If you can get that old machine working you will make me, and a young girl very happy. Her life has been a misery since her last bone marrow transplant and she has been unable to go out. My plan is to teach her how to quilt, if you can fix up that old bird that is. Oh, I've just thought, you'll make three birds happy! Cuppa tea, sweetheart?"
"Yes please, two sugars."

Wow, batteries recharged and off to Paramo in Wadhurst to repair their industrials. They are a firm that makes high-end outdoor gear, part of Nikiwax. From Crowborough I took the Rotherfield road. I squeezed through the always blocked High Street and took the Catt's Hill turning to

Mark Cross, and then up wiggly Faircrouch Lane to their workshop. Christmas music was blaring out as I climbed the steps to the second floor where the machine girls were sewing away. One by one I went through each problem before discussing who had bought what present for who in their canteen. Canteens always take me back to the family firm. I love sitting in them. The banter, humour and idle chat makes minutes pass in seconds. I wished them all Happy Christmas and hit the road.

Funny, at 62 I just keep on rolling. However in the last few years I've noticed a few bits have been dropping off! Still I put my head down and keep going, only having to deal with skinflints now and again. I skipped down to Tidebrook on my way to Mayfield, passing where the fabulously rich Hans Rausing had once lived in his East Sussex home. He was the son of Ruben Rausing who in 1944 invented the TetraPak, a cheap waterproof cardboard alternative to the glass bottle. Legend tells that his eureka moment came while watching his wife Elisabeth, stretching skin, while stuffing sausages on the kitchen table. Some say it made him the richest man in the world. When taxation in Sweden became excessive the clan moved to England. Hans bought a sprawling estate called Wadhurst Park, tucked away in the middle of nowhere and crammed with deer, which he occasionally liked to shoot. Hans bit the dust back in August at the ripe old age of 93. Amazingly legend tells that his extraordinary family have so far given away over a billion pounds to charity.

I dropped down Rushers Cross then passed the mill in Coggins Mill Lane, coming out opposite the old Bishop's Palace in Mayfield. The Bishop's Palace is now a school, which I am occasionally called to when the machines go down. When I first called decades ago, it was run by nuns from the St Leonards & Mayfield Convent, near Bexhill, down on the coast. In their black habits they would flit and fly around the old place like bats on steroids. Along one windy tunnel, between the two main buildings, it always looked like they were trying to take off! Now the school is thriving, with two sewing departments and new enthusiastic staff. I miss the old bats, not the way they could stretch a penny into a pound, but the way I always left with a blessing or two. Take my word for it, nothing puts a smile on your face as quick as being blessed by a nun.

I popped down to Boreham Street to Scolfes for a bite to eat before continuing. Scolfes Tea Rooms are perched over ancient cellars and the previous owner, Jim Bond, once gave me a tour of them. We forget that many old buildings are just as big underneath as they are on top. The old sea port of Winchelsea, along the coast a smidgen, is dotted with pretty cottages, all sitting on huge cellars for wine and beer storage. Jim Bond sold the cafe to concentrate on his hugely successful career as a writer. His Fighting Sail Series, under Alaric Bond, is a worldwide winner. When I pop in to his new home to service Kitty's Singer 500, he often shows me his latest masterpiece. He is our very own local celebrity.

Just after three I noticed that my automatic headlights flicked on. The short winter days were giving us less than seven hours of light. I could see Eastbourne in the distance as I drove by Herstmonceux Castle, down the Wartling Road. With one more call to do I was happy. I had two payments in cash, one BACS electronic transfer payment. One I needed to send an invoice to, and one promise of payment that I might see next year. I just had to hope on that one. I had a pot of lovely local Buxted Honey, six farm eggs, two packs of sausages, and a full stomach. Boy would I be glad to be home. I'd bung my tools in the garage, lock the car and put my feet up in front of the box and watch an old movie. Preferably a black & white one with a faded star no youngster has ever heard of.

My last call of the year was at the wonderful Art Deco Kepplestone Flats in Stavely Road, Eastbourne. Possibly the plushest flats in Eastbourne (besides Pearl Court, built for the directors of Pearl Assurance in Devonshire Place). The road is a nod to the 7th Duke who built our town. I loved researching his life when I wrote my book, Eastbourne, Building A Duke's Dream. Kepplestone was built on the site of an old girls school and oozes money. The multiple entrances have more brass than a Northern mining town's band and as much mahogany as a Cuban logging factory.

I soon found myself sitting at a huge desk with a beautiful bronze dancing girl in Arabian dress to keep me company. Besides it sat a basic but gorgeous Singer model 15 hand crank. In front of me was a large window overlooking the English Channel. The panorama was nothing short of magnificent. The finest flats in Eastbourne, dropping down to a three-tiered promenade that swept into a dark sea, full of grey winter menace. Along the horizon, the Sovereign Lighthouse, that was soon to be dismantled, was doing a fine job of warning passing ships of the dangerous shallow shoals. An enormous cruise ship, lit up like a London department store, was sailing into the darkening sea, probably heading for Southampton or Portsmouth along the coast. There it would dock and pick up 'perfectly preened' passengers before heading for the Mediterranean, or some other exotic destination that I could only dream of.

I sipped a cup of perfectly sweet coffee, slipped on my glasses and got to work. An hour later the Singer was turning like new, making that wonderfully rhythmic 'clackety' sound. All the seizures removed, everything balanced and the tension spot on. I glanced up at the view but it had gone. The window had turned into a black mirror, throwing back a perfect image of an old man sitting at a sewing machine. I smiled and waved. Guess what! He waved back. Mirrors have a way of doing that.

I pulled into my drive and sat for a moment, listening to the quiet rumble of the engine, feeling its warmth blowing on my feet. Another year done and dusted I thought. Sweet Lord don't they fly. 2020 was knocking on the door but before that there was some serious celebrating to do. Now, problem, problem. Which grandchild to tease first!

Whatever time of year you read this tale, Happy Christmas one and all.

Epilogue

God, life is tough isn't it! It's mean, rough, sad and horrible. Daily we are bombarded with every bit of awful human tragedy from around the world. Luckily it is also amazing, fabulous, stimulating, and just gobsmacking. On top of that Mother Nature seems to want to turn us into compost every chance she gets! Yet in the same breath, showers us with beauty and wonder. We think we have some sort of control but no one really knows the future. How we deal with so much piled on us is what makes the Human Race unique and inspiring.

As we all know there are villains in every story who do their best to ruin our lives. In reality, compared to the majority of people on this planet, there is only a tiny percentage of these nasty little people, but boy, they make more noise and trouble than all of us put together. We just put our heads down and trundle on. You only have to look at theatres and concert halls, stadiums and arenas to see that, as a race, we actually love being together and most of the time we all get along great. Many people get a huge surge of energy being in a crowd. Others get their energy from being quietly alone, in peace. It is only occasionally that some nutter kicks off and gets enough press to make us think the world is sliding down the drain.

I've spent a whole life time examining my fellow man. What have I learnt? You guessed it, almost nothing. The first problem is that the longer you live the more awful things you see. But that's not the point of life is it! If you worry about everything, all the time, you lose the most precious gift we have—life itself! What's the point of life if you can't hope and dream? I've learnt that, not counting fate and luck, you seem to get out of life mainly what you put into it, so the harder you chase your dreams the more likely you are to get closer to them. Along the way I've seen that sometimes my worst mistakes have turned out to be my best lessons.

All said and done, Time is the biggest thief you will ever meet. I've had many things stolen from me since I was a kid but nothing's so irreplaceable as time. These last 63 years have passed in about 60 days.

I've also learnt that I can't change the world but I can help some people's worlds. I can tell you for a fact that encouragement is worth its weight in gold, a kind word can resurrect you at your lowest moment and a helping hand, when not asked for, is genuinely priceless. You may ask if that is what makes me smile so often. Not altogether. The sweetest old dear once told me that she had two choices in life; to frown or smile. She looked in the mirror and decided that she was so ugly when she frowned that she would smile! Well, it's worked for me, too.

I can also tell you for a fact that, although we are moulded by our world and our experiences, we are born with our characters. Growing up with five very different brothers taught me that early, and age just confirmed it. Getting old isn't much fun, but it can be funny. Besides all the aches and pains all us oldies succumb to, I find myself doing just the strangest things. When I pick something up now I make the weirdest noises, something like a groaning grunt finishing off with 'whoamumma'! I have the horrible feeling I picked it up from an old Italian builder called Franco. He did some work for me nearly 40 years ago. I used to laugh at him grunting away to himself, now I'm uttering the same strange sounds every time I bend over!

I'll tell you another thing I've learnt. Attitude is everything, it really is. It might not actually be the meaning of life but it is probably the closest thing you will ever get to it. Combine effort with attitude and you have a recipe for success. Anything worth having or making reflects the effort and attitude put into it, from classic cars (or in my case Victorian sewing machines) to relationships. Here is a little test to explain. Tell someone 'I really love you,' in a genuine heartfelt way, maybe with flowers or something they adore. Then do it again, this time with a lazy and sarcastic tone. The effects are completely different, aren't they! That's attitude in a nutshell. Oh but don't do it to the delivery person. They might get the wrong idea!

In 1814, England had been having a severe winter. In London it was so cold that the River Thames froze over. This led to the experts of the day stating that, beyond any doubt, that it was the start of the next Ice Age. They had been expecting it! Britain would slowly get colder and colder and become uninhabitable for around 10,000 years. These cycles had been going on for millennia and there was nothing to be done! Everyone would eventually have to leave or die. What did the Londoners do? They ignored the doom and gloom brigade and had a frost fair on the Thames, even walking an elephant across it for a laugh! Their attitude was positive, compared to the experts negative. How simple and how profound that one word can be. Still don't believe me! Try it for a week and see it change your world forever. Attitude may actually be the single most important thing you can ever learn.

Someone famous once said that we all leave ripples that flow outward, touching other people's worlds. It is my hope that I have in my own small way helped many people. Sweet Lord, if I was paid in kindness in Heaven for being patient with crazy old dears (I know I should be politically correct and call them 'interesting'), I would be laughing, for the first millennia at least.

I still have so many more stories to scribble down. Once again I've missed out Dan and his brilliant story of the Nazis bombing the margarine factory near his home, blowing a billion peanuts into the air. Then there is J K Ross, our very own hero who gave his life fighting in the skies above our war-torn country. Then there was the Parker Pen factory that was just up the road from me in Newhaven. That is a great story waiting to be told. How a small fishing village gave way to the finest pen makers in the world and how almost everyone in the area was somehow connected with the business. And what was happening to their solid gold nibs! So many true stories but the clock is ticking, forever ticking. I hope that my stories are a balance to this crazy complicated world, a calm in the storm of life. Simple tales from the heart to bring a little comfort, even a smile or two.

As many of my readers know I write a lot of academic books on sewing machine history and the pioneers that made it possible. It's a strange fact that I have published more books on the subject than any other person, living or dead. All of my television and Internet appearances have been due to these. There are many more of them than the books on my life and travels. It is my daily life however, that has been such a joy to write down and to relive with my readers. I do hope that you have enjoyed coming along the Sussex lanes with me and meeting my wonderful (you now know I mean crazy, don't you!) customers.

So here we are once again, at the end of another book, another wonderful journey across my beautiful county, scribbled over countless pages. Once more, as the curtain falls, I take my final bow. I wish that life may treat you well. Until the next time my friends, I bid you a fond farewell.

Alex Askaroff
A Sussex Lad, Born & Bred

Astonishingly, this British Bradbury B2, made around 1880, is still in regular use today. If there was wear, even as much as a human hair, it would not work! The quality of engineering by those amazing Victorians often leaves me speechless. The company trademark was the Duke of Wellington. You can just make out his large nose on the machine!

VISIT AMAZON TO SEE A LIST OF ALEX ASKAROFF'S CURRENT BOOKS

Local history entwined with fascinating tales. Evocative and descriptive. Excellent writing—Professor J. Johnson.

Have I Got A Story For You

Alex I. Askaroff

Yet again Alex has woven his magic. I kept saying I never knew that and I'm a local. This may just be one of the best books I've ever read!
J. Vincent

TALES FROM THE COAST
by Alex Askaroff

Tales from the Coast, crammed with original photos, continues the series of short true stories in which Alex Askaroff once again brings both England's history and her people vividly to life. Although they are local stories

Alex's popularity and easy writing style means his books are now available in over 40 countries. They were some of the first books ever on digital media like the Apple iPad and Kindle.

Alex Askaroff, a Sussex lad, left a thriving family business in specialty textiles to become a journeyman, repairing sewing machines, carrying on a trade that he had known since a child. Alex, now a Master Craftsman, has the enthusiasm of a poet and a pure loveof story-telling. As Alex brings sewing machines back to life he also picks up local stories, history and gossip. And what stories they are! All the stories are inspired by the people who actually lived them. These are real people, no media sensations, just ordinary hard working people who, through their long lives, have had fascinating incidents indelibly burned into their memories.

Tales from the Coast celebrates the spirit of Sussex life, its people, colour and vibrancy. Dorothy tells of her years of hop picking even as the Battle of Britain rages overhead, Sheila tells of her encounter with a jaguar in the jungle far from home. Flo tells of her evacuation as a child and her glorious years on the farm, far away from harm.

From the disappearance of Lord Lucan in Uckfield to the Buxted Witch, from William Duke of Normandy, to Queen Elizabeth's dressmaker, Tales from the Coast is crammed with a fascinating mix of true stories that will have you entranced from start to finish.

You may feel that you know Sussex but I guarantee that Alex will provoke you into wanting to look again.
Frank Scutt OBE
Vibrant stories told with skill and humour that provide a valuable insight into a magical part of England.
Alaric Bond. Author
Wonderful humour and writing.
Sussex Life
A polished masterpiece.
What's On Magazine.
I couldn't put it down, Hillarie Belloc would have been happy to put his name to a book like this.
Magnet Magazine
Landscapes and pictures straight from the heart. A fascinating read.
Jim Flegg Country Ways Television

Printed in Poland
by Amazon Fulfillment
Poland Sp. z o.o., Wrocław